AMERICA ★ THE ★ BEAUTIFUL

California

BY TAMRA B. ORR

Third Series

Children's Press®
A Division of Scholastic Inc.
New York ★ Toronto ★ London ★ Auckland ★ Sydney
Mexico City ★ New Delhi ★ Hong Kong
Danbury, Connecticut

CONTENTS

HOLLYWOOD

ROUTE 66

PROJECT ROOM

★

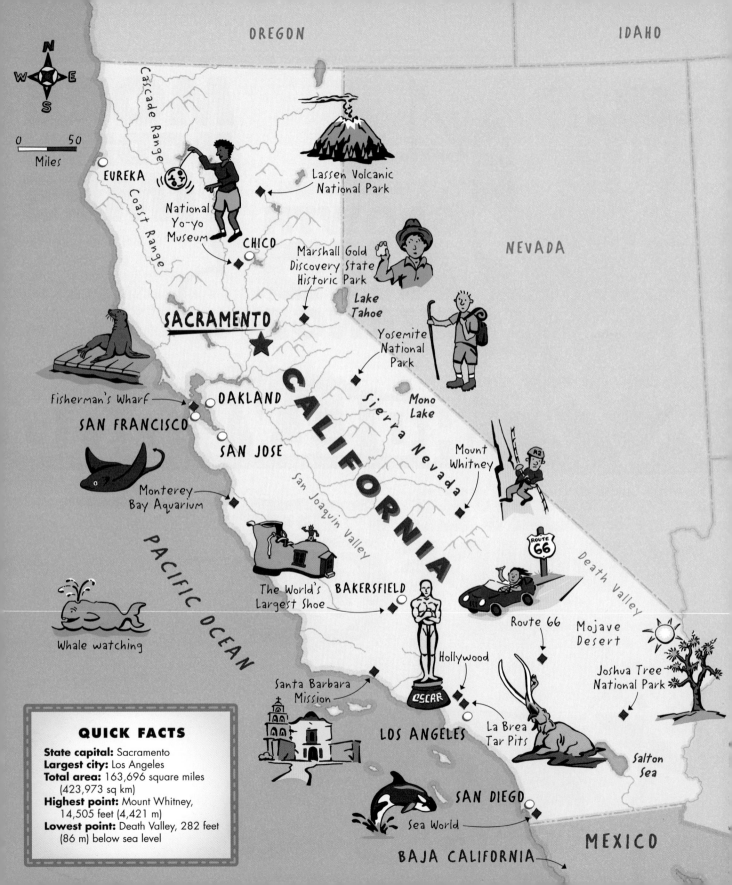

OREGON

IDAHO

NEVADA

NEVADA

MEXICO

BAJA CALIFORNIA

PACIFIC OCEAN

CALIFORNIA

Cascade Range

Coast Range

Sierra Nevada

San Joaquin Valley

Death Valley

EUREKA

CHICO

SACRAMENTO

OAKLAND

SAN FRANCISCO

SAN JOSE

BAKERSFIELD

LOS ANGELES

SAN DIEGO

Lake Tahoe

Mono Lake

Salton Sea

National Yo-yo Museum

Lassen Volcanic National Park

Marshall Gold Discovery State Historic Park

Yosemite National Park

Mount Whitney

Fisherman's Wharf

Monterey Bay Aquarium

Whale watching

The World's Largest Shoe

Santa Barbara Mission

Hollywood

OSCAR

La Brea Tar Pits

Route 66

ROUTE 66

Mojave Desert

Joshua Tree National Park

Sea World

QUICK FACTS

State capital: Sacramento
Largest city: Los Angeles
Total area: 163,696 square miles
(423,973 sq km)
Highest point: Mount Whitney,
14,505 feet (4,421 m)
Lowest point: Death Valley, 282 feet
(86 m) below sea level

N W E S

0   50
Miles

Welcome to California!

HOW DID CALIFORNIA GET ITS NAME?

In 1510, a Spanish novelist wrote about a land called California. He said it was filled with gold and pearls. Beautiful black women warriors lived there. Their queen, Calafía, was the bravest and most beautiful of them all. Explorers, thinking that the story was true, set out to find this fantastic place.

When Hernán Cortés reached Mexico, he sent expeditions northward along the Pacific Coast, hoping to find Calafía's land. Of course, they never found it. Still, Spaniards began calling the coastal territory they explored California.

By 1770, the entire Pacific Coast controlled by Spain had been given the name California. Soon, the Spanish-speaking people who lived there were called Californios. That's how, most historians agree, California got its name!

CALIFORNIA

WYOMING

NEBRASKA

COLORADO

UTAH

ARIZONA

NEW MEXICO

TEXAS

8

READ ABOUT

Hikers, runners,
and other outdoor
enthusiasts enjoy
Mount Whitney. Its
peak is the tallest
in the continental
United States.

LAND LAND LAND LAND LAND

CHAPTER ONE

LAND

★

WHAT WILL YOU FIND IN CALIFORNIA? You name it! It's a place of extremes: Mount Whitney, the highest point in the lower 48 states, soars to 14,505 feet (4,421 meters) above sea level, while Badwater in Death Valley, the lowest point on the North American continent, drops down to 282 feet (86 m) below sea level.

California is the third-largest state. Its 163,696 square miles (423,973 square kilometers) are home to some of the world's tallest trees and to the country's oldest Ice Age fossils, highest waterfalls, and deepest valleys.

CALIFORNIA'S FORMATION

California's gorgeous geology is the result of millions of years of volcanic and tectonic activity. Its magnificent mountain valleys were carved out by glaciers during the ice ages, and they were shaped by ongoing wind and rain. The picturesque coastline of California is continually shaped by the pounding waves of the Pacific Ocean. California has a wealth of mineral resources. These mineral resources include the rich soil of the Central Valley, the gold of the Sierra Nevada, and oil off the coast and in various locations across the state.

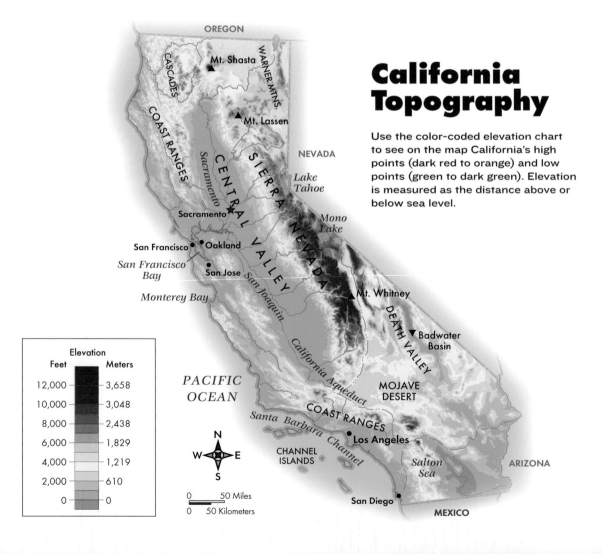

California Topography

Use the color-coded elevation chart to see on the map California's high points (dark red to orange) and low points (green to dark green). Elevation is measured as the distance above or below sea level.

THE GOLDEN STATE

California stretches along the West Coast of the United States, and the Pacific Ocean washes up against its miles and miles of coastline. Overlooking it all are soaring mountain ranges with snow-covered tops that peek through the occasional cloud.

Oregon is at California's northern border. To the east are the states of Nevada and Arizona, and to the west lies the sparkling blue water of the Pacific Ocean. The southern border is home to the Mexican state of Baja California. *Baja* is the Spanish word for "low."

LAND REGIONS

Can you imagine seeing mountains that drop straight into the sea? Or standing in

Big Sur is a sparsely populated region in central California where the Santa Lucia Mountains rise sharply above the Pacific Ocean. The Bixby Creek Bridge, shown here, helped introduce automobile traffic among the coastal towns.

California Geo-facts

Along with the state's geographical highlights, this chart ranks California's land, water, and total areas compared to all other states.

Total area; rank . . . . . . 163,696 square miles (423,973 sq km); third
Land; rank . . . . 155,959 square miles (403,934 sq km); third
Water; rank . . . . 7,736 square miles (20,036 sq km); sixth
   Inland water . . . . 2,674 square miles (6,926 sq km)
   Coastal water . . . . 222 square miles (575 sq km)
   Territorial water . . . . 4,841 square miles (12,538 sq km)
Geographic center . . Madera County, 38 miles (61 km) east of Madera
Latitude . . . . 32° 30′ N to 42° N
Longitude . . . . 114° 8′ W to 124° 24′ W
Highest point . . . . .Mount Whitney, 14,505 feet (4,421 m)
Lowest point . . . . Death Valley, 282 feet (86 m) below sea level
Largest city . . . . Los Angeles
Longest river . . . . Sacramento

Source: U.S. Census Bureau

 The state of Rhode Island could fit inside California more than 130 times!

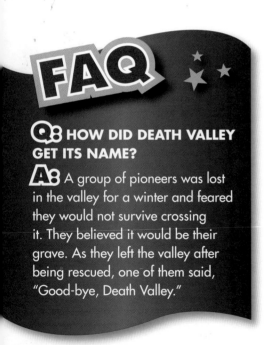

Death Valley is the hottest and driest place in North America.

FAQ

Q: HOW DID DEATH VALLEY GET ITS NAME?

A: A group of pioneers was lost in the valley for a winter and feared they would not survive crossing it. They believed it would be their grave. As they left the valley after being rescued, one of them said, "Good-bye, Death Valley."

the hot desert and looking up at snow-covered mountain peaks? You will see all of that and more in California.

California has four main land regions: the coastal ranges, the desert region, the inland mountains, and the Central Valley. Each one is unique in how it looks and what it has to offer.

The Coastal Ranges

From the rocky cliffs along the northern California coast to the sandy beaches in the south, California boasts one of the world's most spectacular coastlines. Big Sur and Long Beach are favorites with locals and tourists alike.

Some of the world's largest redwood trees are in this region, as well; the tallest towers 379 feet (116 m). A line of mountain ranges separates the coast from the central valley stretching 800 miles (1,287 km) from the state's northwest corner to the Mexican border in the south. This blending of mountains and beaches makes California a very special place.

The Desert Region

While the coast offers more water than you can measure, the desert region in southeastern California is just the opposite. In this region lies Death Valley, the hottest, driest, lowest place in North America.

It stretches over 140 miles (225 km) and reaches into western Nevada. Summer temperatures rise above 120 degrees Fahrenheit (49 degrees Celsius). While cactus and other plants can grow in many parts of the desert, the heat of Death Valley makes vegetation scarce.

The Inland Mountains

Half of California is mountains. The Sierra Nevada was originally formed millions of years ago. This range includes the towering Mount Whitney.

Yosemite National Park is in the Sierra Nevada. There, Yosemite Falls, the highest waterfall in the country, plummets 2,425 feet (739 m). Park inhabitants include wild animals such as black bears, coyotes, and mountain lions, as well as golden eagles, gray owls, and peregrine falcons.

The volcanic peaks of the Cascade Range in northeast and north-central California have formed as **lava** oozed out of the earth's crust and hardened.

Mount Shasta, in the Cascades, is the fifth-highest peak in California. Like other mountains in the area, Shasta is a **dormant** volcano. It soars more than 14,179 feet

WORDS TO KNOW

lava *fiery melted rock*

dormant *not active at present, but could be active at some future time*

Mount Shasta is an inactive volcano that looms up in the Cascade Range.

JOHN MUIR: A TRUE NATURE LOVER

No one loved California's natural beauty more than John Muir (1838–1914)!

Born in Scotland, Muir moved to California in 1868 and spent years exploring its mountain wilderness. He shared his love of nature through his writings, by creating the Sierra Club, and by campaigning to protect wild places for future generations. Without Muir's efforts, national parks such as Yosemite might never have been created.

? Want to know more? See www.johnmuir.org

(4,322 m) above sea level. Poet Joaquin Miller once described it as "white as a winter moon" in the middle of the "great black forests."

The Central Valley

Half of all the fruits, vegetables, and nuts grown in the United States are grown in California's Central Valley. It is the most fertile land in the state. In the region's vineyards, row after row of grapevines cover the ground with bright green leaves. Along with grapes, farms grow tomatoes, squash, peppers, and other crops.

The two longest rivers in the state, the San Joaquin and the Sacramento, flow through the region. Lake Oroville Dam is also here, rising 770 feet (235 m) and extending 6,920 feet (2,109 m) across the Feather River. It is the highest human-made dam in the United States. The dam provides a storage facility for water that is used to irrigate crops in the valley and to produce electricity in hydroelectric power plants.

The Bernardus winery in Carmel Valley is part of the Central Valley, which has fertile soil that is perfect for growing grapes.

PLANT LIFE

Forests cover more than one-third of California. The most famous trees of the coastal forests are the coast redwoods, but the region is also home to the Douglas fir and other evergreens. The world's tallest living tree (so far!) is found in Redwood National Park. Known as Hyperion, it was discovered in the summer of 2006. It measures 379 feet (116 m) tall. Most of the forest trees are **conifers** such as pines and cedars. Southern California's canyons are home to sycamore trees. While many people think of palm trees when they think of Southern California, most of the palm trees there were originally imported. The only native palm is the California fan palm.

The White Mountains east of the Sierra Nevada are home to the famous ancient bristlecone pines. In the western Sierra Nevada, you will find another kind of redwood, the giant sequoia. Many of these huge trees are protected in Sequoia and Kings Canyon National Parks and at Giant Sequoia National Monument.

In California's southern coastal region, many people live in or near **chaparral** areas. The scrub oaks and other shrubs and grasses that grow here burn easily. A small chaparral fire can quickly spread out of control, threatening homes and lives.

The fertile Central Valley was once home to many diverse grasses and wildflowers such as California poppies and lupines. Today, most of the land in this great valley is used for growing many different fruits, vegetables, and nuts.

Even the harsh, dry environment of the desert is home to many kinds of plants. They have found a way to survive the heat and thrive with little water. Here you will find many different cactus plants, such as the cholla and saguaro. The spiky, twisted limbs of the Joshua tree

WORDS TO KNOW

conifers *trees that bear cones*

chaparral *a thicket of dense shrubs, bushes, and small trees*

The General Sherman Tree is the largest living tree (by volume) in the world. It is 275 feet (84 m) tall, and its trunk measures 103 feet (31 m) in circumference. Giant sequoias are among the largest living things in the world.

can be seen in the Mojave Desert, and a national park was even named after this giant member of the lily family. Though most people think of the desert as a dull, barren wasteland, anyone who visits in the springtime will be amazed at its many beautiful flowers.

High on a windswept mountainside in the Inyo National Forest in east-central California is the world's oldest living thing. It is a bristlecone pine that is more than 4,800 years old. It was alive when the pyramids of Egypt were built! This tree in the White Mountains is called Methuselah, after the oldest man in the Bible.

California National Park Areas

This map shows California's national parks, monuments, preserves, and other areas protected by the National Park Service.

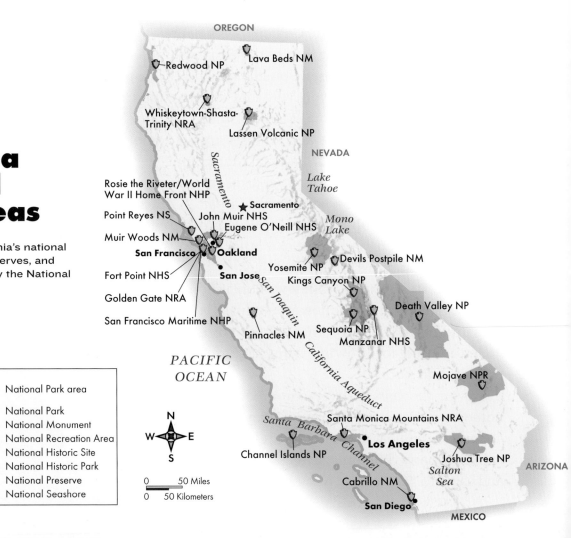

National Park area	
NP	National Park
NM	National Monument
NRA	National Recreation Area
NHS	National Historic Site
NHP	National Historic Park
NPR	National Preserve
NS	National Seashore

ANIMAL LIFE

Plenty of animals live in California's forests and mountains. Squirrels, foxes, and mule deer are common species. Bobcats prefer rocky hillsides that have plenty of brush for cover. Forests provide food, cover, and water for black bears. Mountain lions, or cougars, can be found in coastal forests and deserts. Other animals that were once abundant in California, such as the bighorn sheep, are now endangered. That means they are at risk of dying out if they are not protected.

Thousands of grizzly bears once roamed California's mountains and valleys, but by the late 1800s, hunters had killed almost all of them. In 1889, a grizzly was captured and brought to San Francisco. Named Monarch, it was the model for the bear on the California state flag.

ENDANGERED!

Bighorn sheep, California condors, desert tortoises, black toads, and elf owls were once abundant in California, but their numbers have dwindled. These endangered animals and hundreds of others are now protected in California. The state government works with the federal government, zoos, and other organizations to protect threatened species and increase their populations. The California condor has thrived with this help: in 1982, when they were first protected, there were 22 of these birds in California; in 2006, there were 289, with 138 living in the wild.

The range of bighorn sheep used to cover an area from northern Mexico to Canada. Now they are found only in small pockets of land.

The Mojave Desert is home to some tough animals! They have found ways to survive the heat and get enough food and water. Coyotes travel through the desert at night, and desert bighorn sheep climb its rocky slopes. Big desert tortoises lumber along, looking for grass and flowers to eat. Other desert reptiles include rattlesnakes, desert iguanas, and horned lizards. Eagles and condors soar on the wind currents above the desert's rugged mountains.

On California's coasts, animal life is much different from that in the rest of the state. Each year, between December and April, people gather in many different places overlooking the Pacific Ocean. They pull out their binoculars and take a look. They scan the endless waves. Was that a tail? These people are watching for gray whales to swim by, blowing water out of their spouts. In the winter, these huge creatures begin migrating south from Alaska. They are heading for the warmer waters of Baja California so the females can give birth. In late spring, they migrate north again, this time with their calves by their sides. Seals, sea lions, and sea otters can be spotted along the rocky coasts, as well.

Gray whales can live 50 to 60 years and grow to lengths of 52 feet (16 m). To get an up-close look, these whale-watchers traveled to the warm waters off Baja California where the grays spend the winter months.

California Weather Report

This chart shows record temperatures (high and low) for the state, as well as average temperatures (July and January) and annual precipitation in San Francisco and Los Angeles.

Record high temperature . . . . 134°F (57°C)
   at Greenland Ranch on July 10, 1913
Record low temperature . . . . –45°F (–43°C)
   at Boca on January 20, 1973
Average July temperature, Los Angeles . . . . 69°F (21°C)
Average January temperature, Los Angeles . . . . 57°F (14°C)
Average yearly precipitation, Los Angeles . . . . .13 in. (33 cm)
Average July temperature, San Francisco . . . . 63°F (17°C)
Average January temperature, San Francisco . . . . 49°F (9°C)
Average yearly precipitation, San Francisco . . . . .20 in. (51 cm)

Sources: National Climatic Data Center, NESDIS, NOAA, U.S. Department of Commerce

 **One day, San Andreas Lake got 13.6 inches (34.5 cm) of rain! That is more than half the amount of rain most of the state gets per year.**

CLIMATE

There are five climate regions in California: coastal, valley, foothill, mountain, and desert. Each one is unique. From frigid mountaintops to blazing hot deserts, and from San Francisco's fog to Southern California's warm sunshine, a trip through California offers a sampling of many kinds of weather.

There is an old song that goes, "It never rains in California," and in the state's desert regions, that is almost true! The deserts may see only a couple of inches the entire year. In other parts of the state, rain is much more common, especially in the coastal region. There it can rain up to 100 inches (254 cm) a year.

Even though you may picture only blue skies and warm sun in California, snow is part of the climate, too. A layer of snow can be seen on its highest mountaintops for most of the winter. Several roads can be closed for the entire winter because of heavy snowfall.

There is a reason people flock to California to vacation, of course. Usually, the coastal regions stay warm all year. The farther you go from the coast, however, the more the temperatures change with the seasons.

NATURAL DISASTERS

California boasts sunny days and warm temperatures. But nature can also be harsh here.

During a severe earthquake, buildings can be ruined and entire neighborhoods destroyed. Luckily, most earthquakes are too minor to be felt.

MINI-BIO

KEIITI AKI: EARTHQUAKE EXPERT

In his more than 50 years as a seismologist (a person who studies earthquakes), Keiiti Aki (1930–2005) invented more precise ways to measure quakes with special computer models. These models are used to look for patterns that may help predict where and when big quakes will strike in the future. Aki began studying earthquakes in Japan. He later moved to California to study and teach. Aki went to the University of Southern California in 1991 and founded the school's now-famous Earthquake Center.

Earthquake!

Earthquakes shake California daily. Thousands of quakes can hit in a year. California sits where two major pieces of Earth's crust—the North American Plate and the Pacific Plate—come together. When Earth's molten core oozes and swirls, the miles-thick plates move. When two plates collide against each other or move in different directions, earthquakes happen. Cracks in the earth's crust are called faults. The most famous fault in California is the more than 800 mile (1,287 km) long San Andreas fault.

Most of California's earthquakes are too small to be felt, happening every few minutes around the clock. Others are much bigger. One of the worst was in 1906 in the region around San Francisco. Between 700 and 3,000 people died, many from the chaos and fire that followed the quake. Based on the amount of damage done, this quake had a magnitude of 7.0. Other big quakes in history include a 7.7 in 1952, which hit Kern County, and a 7.1 in 1989, which hit the San Francisco area.

Wildfire!

A crackling noise fills the air. Blue skies turn dark, and clouds are blocked by billowing smoke. Animals and birds rush to get to safety. Lightning or a careless camper has ignited a wildfire!

With its dry terrain and strong winds, California has experienced huge wildfires for years. In 2003, the Cedar Fire spread across the southern portion of the state. It burned 800,000 acres (324,000 hectares), killed 15 people, and destroyed more than 3,400 homes. Damage was estimated at more than $2 billion. In July 2006, another huge wildfire covering 110 square miles (285 sq km) raced through Yucca Valley, destroying hundreds

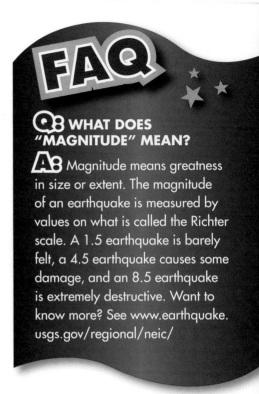

FAQ

Q8 WHAT DOES "MAGNITUDE" MEAN?

A8 Magnitude means greatness in size or extent. The magnitude of an earthquake is measured by values on what is called the Richter scale. A 1.5 earthquake is barely felt, a 4.5 earthquake causes some damage, and an 8.5 earthquake is extremely destructive. Want to know more? See www.earthquake.usgs.gov/regional/neic/

In June 2005, a landslide destroyed more than a dozen homes in Laguna Beach, about 30 miles (48 km) southeast of Los Angeles.

of homes and buildings and forcing Governor Arnold Schwarzenegger to declare a state of emergency. More than 60,000 acres (24,000 ha) were burned, and almost 3,000 firefighters worked to battle the blaze.

Landslide!

Once the immediate danger from wildfires is gone, more trouble can be just around the corner. As soon as rains arrive or winter snows melt, the water rushes down the mountains and—without the trees, bushes, and other greenery to slow it down or soak it up—can create flash floods and mudslides. In 2005, 36 homes were destroyed in the La Conchita landslides. Ten people were killed.

PROTECTING THE ENVIRONMENT

Californians keep working to find better ways to live with nature. They try hard to reduce the amount of garbage they produce. Some people have built wind farms that harvest energy from the wind and reduce the need for oil. Seismologists are learning to forecast earthquakes, and engineers study how to build quake-proof buildings. Some scientists are designing ways to reduce the damage that can result from a landslide or wildfire.

In summer 2006, the U.S. House of Representatives approved a bill that officially protects 273,000 acres (110,000 ha) of coastal mountains, scenic rivers, and forests stretching from California's Napa Valley to the Oregon border. No companies are allowed to log, mine, or drill in the area.

Clearly, California is a land of extremes. From highest to lowest, desert to seashore, sprawling cities to tranquil forests, the state also is a place of contrasts and ongoing change. Natural events such as earthquakes, wildfires, and landslides keep reshaping the land. Of course, development and population growth will keep changes coming, as well.

Californians appreciate their stunning scenery, and they work to protect and preserve their natural places.

READ ABOUT

Petroglyphs are carvings in rocks. Early inhabitants of what is now California created these petroglyphs in the eastern Sierras.

c. 28,000 BCE
Explorers cross the Bering land bridge

▲ c. 9000 BCE
The earliest Californians settle in the region

c. 3000 BCE
The atlatl, or throwing stick, is developed

CHAPTER TWO

FIRST PEOPLE

★

WOULD YOU BELIEVE THAT PEOPLE HAVE BEEN LIVING IN CALIFORNIA FOR MORE THAN 11,000 YEARS? The first explorers most likely came across the Bering land bridge. This strip of land once connected Siberia to Alaska. It has been under water for the last 10,000 years. The travelers had hiked and canoed over countless miles—all the way from Asia!

1000–1600

The Cahuilla occupy the northeast San Diego area

▲ **900** CE

Most native peoples are settled in California

▲ **mid-1500s**

European explorers arrive

WHO WERE THE FIRST CALIFORNIANS?

The very first people to set foot in what is now California had left everything they knew far behind. They were searching for warmer weather and followed the tracks of animals—which they hunted—to a completely new place. In their languages, they called themselves "The People." Today, they are known as Native Americans. The European explorers who followed, however, thought they had landed in Asia. They gave the natives the name *Indians*.

By the time the Europeans arrived in the mid-1530s, there were hundreds of different clans, or large family groups, living throughout the region. Each group had its own culture, with unique traditions and **rituals**. They made and used different kinds of tools, lived in different kinds of houses, and even ate different foods. Each clan also had its own language—and hundreds of different dialects were spoken.

WORD TO KNOW

rituals *religious ceremonies or social customs*

Native Americans often lived in communities that were far away from one another.

Native American Peoples

(Before European Contact)

This map shows the general area of Native American people before European settlers arrived.

FAQ

Q8 HOW DID THE EARLY PEOPLE USE ACORNS?

A8 Usually, the women crushed and ground protein-packed acorns to make a kind of flour. Then, they sifted and washed it to remove its bitter acids. Finally, they baked the flour into bread or boiled it to make a mushy porridge.

The Tipai-Ipai people lived in Southern California and northern Baja California. Some of them lived in caves, while others had dome-shaped homes that were made from poles and covered with thatch or palm leaves. Their diet was made up of whatever they could catch or gather in the forests. They often ate cactus and acorns. In fact, acorns were an essential food of many Native Americans. Acorns grow on oak trees and were gathered by the basketful. The Tipai-Ipai also lived off small game animals, as well as fruits such as cherries, plums, and berries.

Another group in Southern California was the Cahuilla, who settled in the San Bernardino Mountains. They lived in shelters made of brush or in rectangular thatched houses. Their diet was similar to that of the Tipai-Ipai, but they also ate squash and beans. They caught salmon and other fish, which were plentiful in the lakes and streams.

Some groups planted crops. The Mojave and the Yuma lived along the fertile banks of the Colorado River. There they raised corn, beans, and squash. But water was scarce for the Cahuilla of the southeastern desert. They dug deep into the sand to reach it. They used the water to grow corn, squash, beans, and melons.

The Cahuilla lived in diverse environments, from mountain ranges to canyons to desert. They built both rectangular thatched houses and dome-shaped shelters made of brush.

The northwestern part of California, near the Klamath River, was home to the Karok. In this clan, the houses were made of plants and built over earthen pits. The men and older boys spent a lot of time inside the tribe's sweat lodges. These were enclosed structures with fires burning inside. Men gathered inside to sweat in the heat. This was a purifying ritual, cleansing both the body and the mind.

Hundreds of years ago, the area that now includes San Francisco, California, was home to the Miwok and the Ohlone. They lived along the coast in cone-shaped houses supported by poles and covered with bark or grass. The Miwok ate seeds, berries, and roots, as well as deer, elk, and bear. These wild animals roamed the hills, valleys, and plains, and they were a major source of food.

Picture Yourself . . .

Building a Canoe with the Achumawi

Building a canoe took great amounts of both skill and patience. You started by cutting down just the right tree, usually pine. Once the tree was down, you had to wait for at least three months until it dried out. Then, the inside of the trunk had to be removed. It could be cut out by hand or burned out by fire. If it was burned out, you would reach in—carefully—and scrape out the ash with rocks or shells. To keep the entire tree from catching fire, sometimes wet animal skin was put on the outside of the trunk. When it was done, it had to be sturdy enough to hold more than a dozen people—but light enough to be carried to and from the water.

WHO DID WHAT?

In most Native American villages in California (and elsewhere), men and women had special roles that they passed down to the next generation. Men were the hunters and fishers. They made the tools and equipment they needed in daily life. In some areas, they made canoes out of a variety of trees. They made bows and arrows from branches and sharpened rocks. They made throwing sticks, called atlatls, that were used by

SEE IT HERE!

NATIVE AMERICAN HISTORY

The California State Indian Museum in Sacramento has interesting artifacts and exhibits from the hundreds of tribes that once lived here. You can try tools such as the pump drill, used for making holes in shell beads. Or you can check out the mortar and pestle for grinding up those acorns. There are all kinds of baskets, as well as capes, headbands, and headdresses worn by Native American dancers.

hunters to shoot barbed spears with amazing accuracy. And they made animal traps by digging holes in the ground and covering them with logs and branches.

Women collected wild plants, trapped small animals, and cooked meals. In some villages, they made earthenware pots and wove plant fibers into clothing and baskets.

POMO BASKET MAKING

The Pomo are considered the most artistic of California's basket makers. They would use the fibers of certain plants, such as desert willow or black willow, for the basket's foundation. Then, other plants were used to add color. White came from the roots of sedge grasses. Bulrush roots were used for black, and new shoots of the redbud tree produced red.

Basket makers followed many traditions. Before gathering the plants, they commonly would make some kind of offering. Perhaps they would place acorns or herbs on the ground and burn them as they prayed. Then, as they picked each plant, they would tell the

For some Native Americans, baskets were important for everyday activities as well as in ceremonies.

Creator and the plant what they were using it to make. Often, the weavers included a deliberate flaw in the design—maybe a spot of color where it didn't belong. This is called a spirit door. It lets good spirits in and bad spirits out. Native American basket makers passed their knowledge of this craft down to their children for many generations.

Long ago, baskets were necessary to daily life. Native Americans used them for carrying plants and for storing and serving food. Some baskets were woven so tight that they were used for carrying water. Red-hot rocks were added to the baskets for cooking soup. A baby's cradle was often a basket. Every basket was—and still is—made to contain the basket maker's prayers and to offer spiritual energy to those who used it. No wonder a good basket weaver was such a respected person!

SUSAN BILLY: BASKET WEAVER

Susan Billy (1951–), a contemporary Pomo basket maker, views basket making as a spiritual path. "Among our people, both men and women were basket makers," she explains. "Everything in our lifestyle was connected to these baskets. Our lives were bound the ways baskets were bound together." Billy, who has exhibited her baskets in many museums, learned the craft from her great-aunt Elsie Allen, who was known as a great artist and teacher. Now Billy is carrying on her aunt's work.

LIFE AFTER THE EUROPEANS

When the Spanish explorers arrived, there were about 300,000 Native Americans in California. By 1845, that number was cut by more than half. Only about 30,000 were left in 1870. And by 1900, only about 16,000 remained.

For many centuries and generations, Native Americans had lived in peace with nature and, generally, with one another. However, life had changed. Traders and settlers came from Russia, Spain, Mexico, and the United States. Many Native Americans died of new diseases, while others were driven from their homes.

READ ABOUT

These are ruins from Mission San Luis Rey de Francia. Located in Oceanside, this mission was founded in 1798.

1542 ▲
Juan Rodríguez Cabrillo explores San Diego Bay

1602
Sebastián Vizcaíno reaches the California coast

1769 ►
Junípero Serra establishes the first mission at San Diego

CHAPTER THREE

EXPLORATION AND SETTLEMENT

★

FROM THE EARLY 1500s UNTIL THE EARLY 1800s, CALIFORNIA AND MEXICO WERE PART OF A SPANISH COLONY CALLED NEW SPAIN. The Spanish found rich silver mines in Mexico, but for centuries they ignored California because they didn't believe the land was rich. It wasn't until the 1760s that the Spanish turned their attention northward.

1775
San Diego mission revolt

1821
California becomes part of Mexico

1834 ▶
Mexico begins seizing missions and shutting them down

EARLY EUROPEAN EXPLORERS

The Spanish wanted to secure the border of New Spain, and they wanted to be sure that other Europeans did not take control of their territory first. The era of European exploration was ready to begin! The Native Americans would ultimately pay the heaviest price for this.

Juan Rodríguez Cabrillo was the first European to explore California's Pacific coast. In 1542, he sailed from the Spanish **colony** of Mexico into San Diego Bay. Thinking he had reached the fabled island of California, he claimed it for Spain. Cabrillo's ships may have continued up the coast as far as present-day Oregon.

England got an early peek at California, too. In 1579, the English explorer Sir Francis Drake sailed into a bay on the northern California coast, where he met with the Miwok. He named this land New Albion and claimed it for England before sailing on.

Another Spaniard, Sebastián Vizcaíno, explored the coast in 1602. He reached Monterey Bay and made detailed maps of the coastal area, giving names to many sites. But he didn't find gold or silver, so he couldn't convince the Spanish government to send any settlers

As time went on, Russians started hunting sea animals along the Pacific coast south of Alaska. In 1765, Russian trappers were spotted as far south as present-day San Francisco. This worried the Spaniards. What if Russia invaded this land and claimed it? It was time for Spain to make settlements there.

WORD TO KNOW

colony *a territory claimed by the country that settles it*

Exploration of California

The colored arrows on this map show the routes taken by explorers and pioneers between 1542 and 1846, with some of the old missions where they stopped.

OREGON

Fort Jones

Pit

Fort Crooks

Klamath

Fort Reading

Eel

Sacramento

Feather

Lake Tahoe

NEVADA

Cache

Russian

Fort Ross

San Francisco Solano

Sutter's Fort (Sacramento)

San Francisco Bay

Yerba Buena

Merced

Mono Lake

Owens

San Francisco de Asís

San José de Guadalupe

Monterey Bay

Fort Miller

Fort Monterey

San Carlos Borromeo

Salinas

Kings

San Antonio de Padua

San Luís Obispo de Tolosa

Fort Tejon

PACIFIC OCEAN

Santa Barbara

San Gabriel Arcángel

Los Angeles

San Juan Capistrano

Salton Sea

Colorado

ARIZONA

San Diego de Alcalá

MEXICO

N W E S

0   50 Miles
0   50 Kilometers

Juan Rodríguez Cabrillo, 1542–1543
Francis Drake, 1579
Sebastián Vizcaíno, 1602–1603
Jedediah Smith, 1826–1829
John Frémont, 1842–1844
John Frémont, 1845–1846
Spanish mission
Fort
Present-day state of California

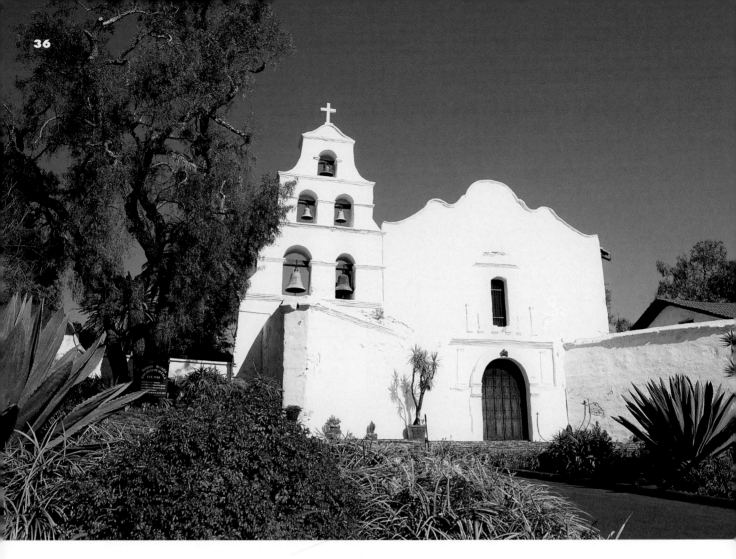

Mission San Diego de Alcalá was established by Father Junípero Serra in 1769. It is California's oldest church.

WORD TO KNOW

missions *places where people teach their religion to others*

PRESIDIOS, MISSIONS, AND PUEBLOS

In 1769, Spain sent a military expedition into California. Led by Gaspar de Portolá, the group included a Roman Catholic *padre*, or priest, Father Junípero Serra. They were to build presidios, or military forts, along the coast to protect settlers. They were also to build **missions.** There, the padres would convert the Native Americans to Christianity, and teach them farming, ranching, and various trades, as well as the Spanish language.

They turned north from Mexico—some by ship and some overland. In the sweltering heat, with no road to follow, the travelers hacked out a trail as they went along. It was a rough journey, and many died along the way. Finally, they reached San Diego. There, in July 1769, Father Serra established Mission San Diego de Alcalá, and Portolá built a presidio. This was the first Spanish settlement in present-day California.

At first, there were only a few isolated missions. Eventually, the Spanish built a chain of missions in California. The trail that connected them was called El Camino Real, Spanish for The King's Highway. By 1823, there were 21 missions linking the coast and four presidios. In addition, the Spanish government encouraged a few hundred settlers to move to California and build small towns, or pueblos. These pueblos would grow to become some of California's largest cities, such as Los Angeles, and San Jose.

JUNÍPERO SERRA: CALIFORNIA'S MOST FAMOUS MISSIONARY

Born in Spain, Junípero Serra (1713–1784) was a Roman Catholic priest. It was Serra's dream to become a missionary, and in 1750, he was sent to New Spain to work among the Indians. He founded the first nine California missions before his death, and others carried on after him. In 1988, the Catholic Church beatified Serra, which is a step toward official sainthood. This caused controversy among those who believe the mission system was cruel and destructive.

MISSION LIFE

The missionaries believed they were serving God by bringing Christianity and European education to the native people. But the Native Americans did not necessarily want or need a new way of life forced on them.

The centerpiece of a mission was the church, with its tall bell tower. Other mission buildings were workshops, kitchens, sleeping quarters, and storehouses. All were built around a square courtyard. Surrounding the mission were vast lands for grazing cattle and sheep and for growing fruits and vegetables.

The trail linking the missions, El Camino Real, became the route of California's scenic Highway 101.

Native American women and children made goods for the missions, such as baskets and rope.

In the missions, Native Americans worked hard and had to follow strict rules. Everyone was taught a trade that contributed to mission life. Men learned to make bricks and wine, to shoe horses, and to turn animal hides into leather. They constructed buildings and tended the cattle and fields. Women wove cloth, made pottery, washed clothes, and cooked meals.

Many missions became thriving communities. They sold goods to Spanish traders, who filled their ships with hides, animal fat, and leather goods from the missions. All profits went to the mission communities, and none to individual Indians no matter how hard they worked.

OBEY—OR ELSE!

While the missionaries may have thought they were improving the lives of the Indians, many Native Americans had a wretched time in the missions. They labored long and hard, with little or no reward.

The punishments for breaking mission rules could be severe. The missionaries believed that Indians needed to live at the mission so they wouldn't forget what they were learning about Christianity. But the Indians couldn't understand why they had to stay.

Some Indians escaped, only to be captured, returned to the missions, and then beaten. Other Indians fought back. In 1775, Indians attacked the San Diego mission. Soldiers from the presidio quickly put down the revolt, however.

Mission life was tough but disease was even tougher. Smallpox, influenza, and even the common cold could infect hundreds, and wipe out entire communities.

Before the Spaniards arrived, as many as 300,000 Indians had lived in California. But thousands died of diseases the Spaniards brought. Others died in conflicts with Spanish soldiers. By 1840, only about 100,000 Indians survived. For most, their ancient languages and cultures were lost.

Picture Yourself . . .

in a Spanish Mission

If you were a Native American child living in a Spanish mission, you probably would attend the mission school. There, you would learn Spanish, which was very different from your own language. You would be taught about Christianity, which was different from your own spiritual beliefs.

In your spare time, you might play traditional Indian games such as stickball. But life in the missions was hard. You would see your family change. Your parents would no longer have control over your life—instead, the missionaries would. Traditional healers could not treat the new diseases. For you and the other children, it was a confusing and difficult time.

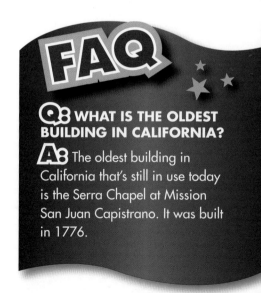

FAQ

Q8 WHAT IS THE OLDEST BUILDING IN CALIFORNIA?

A8 The oldest building in California that's still in use today is the Serra Chapel at Mission San Juan Capistrano. It was built in 1776.

HOW LOS ANGELES BEGAN

How did the thriving city of Los Angeles come to be? In 1781, King Carlos III of Spain decided that a town should be built on the site of a beautiful river—what is now known as the Los Angeles River. The new governor of California, Felipe de Neve, drew up plans and gathered some Mexican and African American families to settle there.

These settlers (11 men, 11 women, and 22 children) gathered on September 4, 1781, at San Gabriel mission. Along with a military escort and two mission priests, they set out for the site. The little town received the name El Pueblo de Nuestra Señora Reina de los Ángeles Sobre El Río Porciuncula (The Town of Our Lady Queen of the Angels on the Porciuncula River). It later became known as Los Angeles.

END OF AN ERA

In New Spain, people were growing tired of Spanish rule. They fought the Mexican Revolution and won independence in 1821. California became part of Mexico.

Now free of Spain, Mexican officials wanted to end the missions, too. In 1834, Mexico began seizing the missions and shutting them down. Mission lands were divided up and given to leading Mexican citizens.

With no reward for their labors, the Indians were sent on their way. Some worked for the new landowners, while others tried to return to their traditional homelands. After less than 70 years, the mission system had come to an end. Today, many missions chapels are active Catholic churches and have museums that are open to the public.

In 1852, after California became a U.S. territory, more than a dozen treaties were put into place that set aside 8.5 million acres (3.4 million ha) throughout the

By 1850, the population of Los Angeles had grown to 1,610.

state for the remaining Native Americans to live on. What happened then? Somehow, the U.S. Senate lost the treaties—and so the Native Americans lost their land. It was not until 1906 that these papers were found again. More than 50 reservations were set up for the Native Americans—but most reservations are in places that are so dry, isolated, and desolate that no one wants to live there.

Today, California has more than 100 government-recognized reservations. As of July 2004, there were 687,400 Native Americans and Native Alaskans living in California, more than in any other state.

Many of the reservations created for Native Americans were located in dry and isolated areas.

42

READ ABOUT

Between 1850 and 1860, California's population increased by more than 300 percent.

1841
The first group of U.S. settlers reaches California by land

▲**1846**
The Bear Flag Revolt takes place

CALIFORNIA REPUBLIC

▲**1848**
Gold is discovered at Sutter's Mill

GROWTH AND CHANGE

★

S TARVING AND IN TATTERED CLOTHES, THE FIRST ORGANIZED U.S. SETTLERS ARRIVED IN CALIFORNIA FROM MISSOURI IN 1841. Some were on horseback. Others were on foot, their wagons left far behind. They were chasing rumors of rich farmland spread by earlier adventurers.

▲ **1850**
California becomes a state

▲ **1869**
The Transcontinental Railroad is completed

1890
California's population exceeds 1 million

JEDEDIAH SMITH: LEADING THE WAY

Jedediah Smith (1799–1831) covered more territory than any other mountain man of his time. He explored the Rocky Mountains, the Sierra Nevada, and the Mojave Desert, making trails that future travelers would follow. While he and his men were walking through the desert, the heat would become so intense that they couldn't stand it. They would bury themselves in sand to keep cool until the sun began to set and the temperatures dropped.

? Want to know more? See http://xroads. virginia.edu/~hyper/HNS/Mtmen/jedesmith.html

WHY DID THEY COME?

When the first U.S. settlers came, California was still part of Mexico. There were no roads and no cities. No one knew there would be gold here. It took a lot of courage to make this journey!

Some of the new explorers were mountain men, rough outdoorsmen who had the necessary skills for surviving the harsh conditions of the wilderness. The seemingly endless

The first organized group of settlers arrived in California in 1841. Many others followed, attracted by stories of California's terrain and climate.

While some made the journey by ship, many of California's first U.S. settlers crossed thousands of miles of rugged terrain by wagon.

acres of forested mountains in the West were teeming with fur-bearing animals. Fur companies wanted those pelts and were more than happy to hire these mountain men to get them.

News about California spread soon after the first pioneers arrived. Reports said the place had a great climate and that land was free for the taking. To people in the east and midwest, California seemed like the perfect place to live.

Settlers soon loaded up their wagons and headed west, whether

MINI-BIO

JAMES BECKWOURTH: TRAIL MAKER

African American James Beckwourth (1798–1866) was one of the first mountain men to publish colorful stories about his experiences. Born in Virginia, he headed west and worked as a guide for the fur traders and the U.S. Army. Captured by Crow Indians, he spent nearly eight years with them, rising to the level of war chief. By the time of the gold rush, he had forged a trail that he advertised as the lowest (and easiest) pass across the Sierra Nevada. Thousands of gold seekers traveled what is still known as Beckwourth Pass.

 Want to know more? See www.beckwourth. org/Trail/

THE DONNER PARTY

It was the winter of 1846–1847, and a group of families from Iowa and Illinois were on their way to the "promised land" of California.

They took a wrong route. Then their oxen died of thirst or ran away in the Salt Lake Desert. Nearly out of food and water, they paused to rest in the Sierra Nevada. Then it began to snow. The group's journey was doomed. Trapped by the snow, they starved.

The rest of the story is unimaginably gruesome. Of the 89 pioneers who started the trip, only 48 survived. You can read all about it in the diaries of Patrick Breen, a member of the Donner Party (so named because the Donner family was among the group). Breen kept a record of his experience. You can see his diary at www.pbs.org/wgbh/amex/donner/sfeature/sf_diary.html

WORDS TO KNOW

adobe *bricks made of sun-dried clay; also, a house made with these bricks*

tallow *hard fat from the bodies of cattle or other animals*

they knew how to get to California or not. As one traveler wrote, they had "no guide, no compass, nothing but the sun to direct them."

While the pioneers fought incredible odds to make their journeys, Native Americans were affected terribly by the westward expansion. As more and more newcomers arrived, the Native Americans saw their land and their way of life taken away. They were pushed out or killed by guns or disease.

DOWN ON THE RANCHO

Native Americans weren't the only ones living in California when the U.S. settlers arrived. There were many Mexicans and people of Spanish descent.

Many Mexicans lived on huge farms called *ranchos*. Juan Francisco Dana grew up on a California rancho. His family's land, near Mission San Luis Obispo, had once belonged to Spain. Dana's rancho covered 38,000 acres (15,300 ha). Each rancho family lived in a house called an **adobe**. They grew crops and raised thousands of sheep and cattle. The sheep produced wool and meat. Cattle yielded meat, hides, and **tallow**. The tallow was made into soap and candles.

Many of the rancho workers were Native Americans who cooked, planted the crops, and cared for the ranch animals. Grizzly bears were so numerous that scarecrows were put up in the fields to try and scare them away.

On June 14, 1846, American rebels demanded that California be free from Mexican rule. They then raised the Bear Flag in front of the Mexican governor's home.

THE BEAR FLAG REVOLT

Settlers from all parts of the United States started pouring into California. While in many ways it seemed like paradise, many of the people were not happy with certain elements. The U.S. settlers believed that the Mexican landowners, known as Californios, had already claimed much of the best farmland. The Mexicans were not happy, either. They were there first and wanted the U.S. settlers to go away.

On June 14, 1846, 33 Americans pounded on the front door of Mexican governor General Mariano Vallejo's house. They demanded that he surrender

Mariano Vallejo was imprisoned by rebels for two months following the Bear Flag Revolt. He later served in California's first senate.

to them because they wanted California to be free of Mexican rule. To their surprise, Vallejo opened the door wearing his uniform and asked them in for breakfast.

The group was further shocked when Vallejo agreed that California should be independent from Mexico. But they did not trust the man, so they arrested him and sent him to Sutter's Fort to be watched over carefully. Once he was gone from the house, the rebels were not sure what to do next. Should they loot the governor's house? One of the leaders discouraged the idea, saying, "Choose ye this day what you will be! We are robbers, or we must be conquerors!" This was the beginning of the independent California Republic. William Todd, nephew of the wife of future president Abraham Lincoln, designed a flag with a grizzly bear and a star on it. Beneath them were the words *California Republic*. The rebels raised the Bear Flag in front of Vallejo's home.

THE MEXICAN-AMERICAN WAR

Send a message today and someone gets it right away. Things were quite different in the 1800s. Messages traveled by land or sea, so people usually did not get them for weeks. That is just what happened to the Bear Flag rebels. When they declared California's independence from Mexico, they had not heard an important piece of news: Mexico and the United States were at war!

The two countries had been threatening each other for years. Both countries wanted the land that would become the western United States. In May 1846, they finally declared war.

Back in Sonoma, the California Republic now had a president—William Ide. But on July 11, U.S. Army captain John C. Fremont marched in and took control. Down came the Bear Flag and up went the U.S.

flag. The California Republic had existed for less than a month. The philosophy known as manifest destiny took over. Manifest destiny is the belief that the United States had the right to expand across the North American continent regardless of who might already be there. This belief was used by the U.S. government to justify taking western lands from Native peoples and from European control.

THINK ABOUT IT!

Manifest Destiny

PRO

John L. O'Sullivan coined the phrase *manifest destiny* when he presented a defense for America's never-ending claim to new territories. In 1845, he wrote about "the right of our manifest destiny to overspread and to possess the whole of the continent which Providence has given us for the development of the great experiment of liberty and federated self-government entrusted to us."

CON

In contrast, in 1837, William E. Channing wrote, "We are a restless people, prone to encroachment, impatient of the ordinary laws of progress. . . . We boast of our rapid growth, forgetting that, throughout nature, noble growths are slow. . . . It is full time that we should lay on ourselves serious, resolute restraint. Possessed of a domain, vast enough for the growth of ages, it is time for us to stop in the career of acquisition and conquest."

The United States won the Mexican-American War in 1848. Peace terms were set forth in the Treaty of Guadalupe Hidalgo. Mexico had to give up an enormous area of land. The United States took control of present-day California, Nevada, and Utah, as well as parts of Colorado, Arizona, New Mexico, and Wyoming. The country now stretched all the way to the Pacific Ocean, and California became an official U.S. territory.

Nearly 7,000 troops were involved in the Battle of Palo Alto in the Mexican-American War. More than 13,000 Americans died in the war.

California: From Territory to Statehood

(1848–1850)

This map shows the original California territory and the area (in yellow) that became the state of California in 1850.

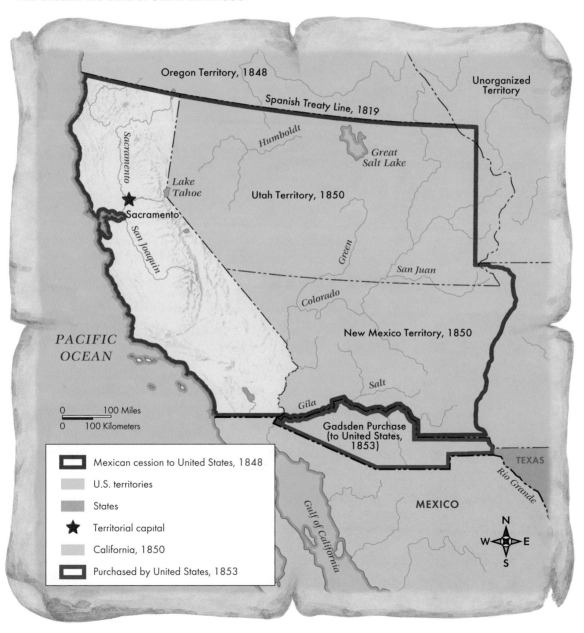

Oregon Territory, 1848

Spanish Treaty Line, 1819

Unorganized Territory

Humboldt

Great Salt Lake

Sacramento

Lake Tahoe

Utah Territory, 1850

Sacramento

San Joaquin

Green

San Juan

PACIFIC OCEAN

Colorado

New Mexico Territory, 1850

Salt

Gila

Gadsden Purchase (to United States, 1853)

TEXAS

Rio Grande

0   100 Miles
0   100 Kilometers

Mexican cession to United States, 1848

U.S. territories

States

★ Territorial capital

California, 1850

Purchased by United States, 1853

Gulf of California

MEXICO

N
W   E
S

John Sutter's mill, the site where gold was first discovered by James Marshall in 1848

FAQ ★ ★ ★

Q: DID MARSHALL AND SUTTER STRIKE IT RICH?

A: No! When news of the discovery spread, workers left Sutter's Mill in search of gold, until eventually the mill was deserted. As a result, Sutter's business failed and he died a poor man. Marshall unsuccessfully tried to charge miners who mined in Coloma and never gained wealth from his discovery. He, too, died poor in 1885.

GOLD FEVER!

January 24, 1848, started out as just an ordinary day for James Marshall. He was building a sawmill for his boss, John Sutter. The mill stood on the American River, near Coloma, in the foothills of the Sierra Nevada. Every morning, Marshall checked on the work done the night before. But this morning was different. He noticed some shiny specks in the rushing water. Then he found even bigger chunks of shiny metal. Sure enough, they turned out to be gold!

Marshall tried to keep his discovery a secret. He didn't want to share the wealth! But the secret leaked out. By 1849, rumors of the gold strike spread like wildfire. Thousands of miners—called 49ers—rushed in from all over the world. The great California gold rush was on!

As people swarmed into California, cities sprang up overnight. Little towns such as San Francisco and Sacramento exploded into big cities. Between 1849 and 1850, the state's population grew from about 15,000 to almost 100,000. Now, California was too important to be just a territory. On September 9, 1850, it became the 31st U.S. state.

MINERS FROM ALL OVER THE WORLD

People of all backgrounds raced to California. They were hoping to strike it rich. The first 49ers sailed from other ports on the Pacific Ocean. Adventurous young men—and a few women—arrived from Chile, Peru, Mexico, and even Hawaii.

Chinese gold seekers arrived in great numbers and soon made up about one-fifth of the mining population. Some of the Chinese immigrants took jobs as cooks, launderers, and merchants, hoping to return to China with a small fortune. However, they faced low pay and unfair hiring practices. They also had to pay the monthly foreign miners' license tax, which was often more than what they earned.

A Chinese man walks to the California gold mines. The prospect of finding gold drew people from all over the world to the state.

54

MINI-BIO

MIFFLIN WISTAR GIBBS: ACTIVIST AND EDITOR

Mifflin Wistar Gibbs (1823–1915) was born in Philadelphia and went to San Francisco during the gold rush. He was an African American **abolitionist** who helped organize the First State Convention of Colored Citizens of California, in 1855. The goal was to fight for equal rights, including the right to vote. He also served as editor of *Mirror of the Times*, an abolitionist newspaper.

? Want to know more? See www.sfmuseum.org/hist6/blackrights.html

WORDS TO KNOW

abolitionist *a person who works to end slavery*

fugitive *a person who tries to flee or escape*

In 1841, African Danish American William Leidesdorff sailed his schooner *Julia Ann* into Yerba Buena, which was about to become San Francisco. By 1848 he was perhaps the most important local citizen. He owned a huge amount of its real estate, built its first hotel, started its first public school, introduced its first horse race, and launched its first steam-powered ship. He died of typhus on the eve of the gold rush. But soon, the lots he had bought for under $100 were worth thousands of dollars, and his estate was valued at more than $1 million.

By 1852, more than 2,000 African Americans traveled to California. Many of them arrived as slaves, even though California was a Free State. This means that slavery was not legal, but such laws were not enforced during the gold rush. Then, the state legislature passed a **fugitive** slave law, which forbade slaves to escape from their masters. So African Americans in California lived under a constant threat of arrest. They also could not testify in court or send their children to public schools.

California's gold rush brought together people from all over the world and from all walks of life. William Perkins, a merchant from Canada, described the mining town of Sonora in 1849: "Here were to be seen people of every nation in all varieties of costume, and speaking 50 different languages, and yet all mixing together amicably and socially." Groups that would previously have remained separate suddenly were living

Panning for gold in California. Many people moved to mining camps with dreams of wealth, but few struck it rich.

and working in close proximity. They were of different races, religions, and languages, yet they all shared the desire to find their fortune.

But life in the mining camps was difficult. According to a staff writer at the *Sacramento Bee*, "one in every five miners who came to California in 1849 was dead within six months." The daily diet was mostly salt pork, biscuits, and molasses. Miners lived in tents and some log cabins. And every camp seemed to have a saloon, where fighting and gambling were common.

Each morning, the miners took their shovels, picks, and pans down to the closest river or stream, rolled up their sleeves, and dipped their pans into the water.

Prospectors search for gold in
Spanish Flat, California.

They hoped to see flecks of gold that would change
their lives.

Although a few people did strike it rich and find
a good amount of gold, most people spent all of their
money on tools, clothing, and food—and found vir-
tually no gold. They usually had to go back home or
look for other ways to make money. Some of the most
successful people were those who opened up stores
that provided the supplies eager '49ers needed. When

Sam Brannon (1819–1889), heard about the gold, he bought every pickax, pan, and shovel he could find. Then, he ran through the streets of San Francisco yelling that gold had been found and selling his wares. Because Brannon was the only one they could buy supplies from, he made $36,000 in just over two months—that's more than most any '49er would ever earn.

San Francisco grew so rapidly, abandoned ships were used as warehouses and hotels.

LEVI STRAUSS: BLUE JEANS MAN

Levi Strauss (1829–1902) headed to California during the gold rush. He set up a general store in San Francisco. One day, a customer told Strauss about a cotton fabric he used to make sturdy pants for his workers. He added metal rivets at certain places on the material to make the pants even stronger. He wondered if Strauss might be interested in going into business making these pants together. Strauss said yes! A new American tradition—denim blue jeans—was born.

? **Want to know more?** See http://www.levistrauss.com/Heritage/History.aspx

These Chinese laborers helped build a railroad for the Loma Prieta Lumber Company, around 1885.

WORD TO KNOW

transcontinental *crossing an entire continent, or landmass between oceans*

THE TRANSCONTINENTAL RAILROAD

Even after the gold rush, newcomers kept pouring into California, but the journey was rough. They could get there only by ship, on horseback, by stagecoach, or wagon and the trip could take months. California needed railroads to move more people faster. Two companies joined forces to build a **transcontinental** railroad. It would stretch from Sacramento all the way to the eastern United States.

In California, the Central Pacific Railroad brought in thousands of workers from China to help build the railroad. From sunrise to sunset, they did dangerous, backbreaking labor. Many Chinese workers died building the railroad.

At last, in 1869, the Transcontinental Railroad was finished. Some of the surviving Chinese workers settled in California towns, often creating their own Chinatown districts. They opened businesses and raised their families. But they were targets of prejudice. In 1882, the U.S. Congress passed the Chinese Exclusion Act, barring Chinese immigration. It would be many years before the ban was lifted.

Meanwhile, California kept growing. By 1890, its population had passed the 1 million mark. Many new settlers were thriving. They started vegetable farms, planted orange groves, and opened ranches. For them, California was truly a land of opportunity.

MOVING AHEAD

In the 1910s and 1920s, a new wave of pioneers arrived in California. This group traveled in automobiles. Some took the Lincoln Highway—the nation's first transcontinental highway, which was built a mere 44 years after the completion of the Transcontinental Railroad. It stretched from New York City to San Francisco.

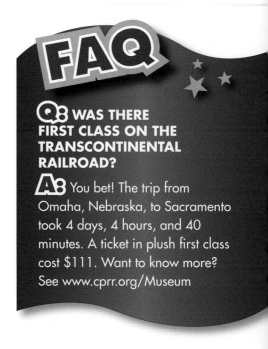

Q8 WAS THERE FIRST CLASS ON THE TRANSCONTINENTAL RAILROAD?

A8 You bet! The trip from Omaha, Nebraska, to Sacramento took 4 days, 4 hours, and 40 minutes. A ticket in plush first class cost $111. Want to know more? See www.cprr.org/Museum

When the Transcontinental Railroad was completed in 1869, getting to California was a lot easier.

READ ABOUT

When many new
residents traveled
to California, they
got there by taking
historic Route 66.

▲ **1906**
*A major earthquake and
fire destroy San Francisco*

1926 ▲
Route 66 opens

1943 ▲
*The Zoot Suit
Riots break out*

CHAPTER FIVE

MORE MODERN TIMES

★

THE NEW CENTURY WAS A TIME OF MASSIVE PROGRESS AND CHANGE IN CALIFORNIA. People were still flocking to this sunny state, but this time it was not in search of land or gold. Instead, it was for good weather, more job opportunities, or the chance to become a movie star. Trains still came through, but most people arrived by car. Route 66 was built to help people cross from one side of the country to the other.

1962

The National Farm Workers Union is founded

1970s

California becomes a leader in computers and other electronics

2007 ▲

Nancy Pelosi becomes the first female speaker of the U.S. House of Representatives

A SHAKY BEGINNING

The morning of April 18, 1906, was not a quiet one as usual. San Franciscans awoke to find their city in chaos. A violent earthquake shook them from their beds, toppled buildings, and left gaping holes in the streets. Gas mains ruptured, stoves toppled, broken power lines sparked, and fires soon raged throughout the city. The fires burned for three full days and were difficult to combat because the water supply was also disrupted. By the time the dust had settled, as many as 3,000 people had been killed and 200,000 people were homeless. Scientists have studied recordings of the 1906 seismic waves. They estimate that the earthquake had a magnitude of about 7.9.

This was one of the worst natural disasters in history, but San Franciscans soon rebuilt their city. In 1915, they showed off their recovery by hosting the Panama-Pacific Exposition, a spectacular world's fair.

Many buildings in San Francisco were damaged by the 1906 earthquake. Some were reduced to rubble.

TRAVELING THE ROADWAYS

Once Route 66 opened in 1926, the mostly rural West was suddenly more accessible from the densely populated Midwest and Northeast. Soon cars full of families moving to California—and trucks full of goods, including many military supplies—covered the highway.

In California, freeways and bridges were springing up everywhere to accommodate all the traffic created by these new residents and industries. The larger cities, such as Los Angeles and San Francisco, were soon full of branching and encircling networks of roads and bridges.

By the beginning of the 21st century, roads and highways were so crowded with automobiles that the government encouraged carpooling and the use of trains, buses, and other public transportation. Within just 30 years, California's population would grow from 1.5 million to 5.7 million. It was the place to be!

HOLLYWOOD, HERE I COME

Imagine life without TV or movies. In the very early 1900s, people were just starting to experiment with moving pictures. Soon the country fell in love with watching films. The 1920s through the 1940s is called the Golden Age of Hollywood. Companies such as

SHIRLEY TEMPLE BLACK: GOLDEN GIRL

People just loved her blond curls, and she tap-danced her way into America's hearts. Shirley Temple (1928—) was born in Santa Monica and became one of the most famous child stars ever. Young Shirley Temple appeared in dozens of films in the 1930s and 1940s. And she was paired with stars such as Bill "Bojangles" Robinson, Gary Cooper, and Carole Lombard.

Later in life, she married businessman Charles Alden Black. And she became involved in politics. President Richard Nixon appointed her as a delegate to the United Nations. And she later served as U.S. ambassador to the countries of Ghana and Czechoslovakia.

? Want to know more? See *Shirley Temple Black: Child Star and Diplomat* by Jean Blashfield Black (Chicago: Ferguson Publishing, 2000).

FAQ

Q8 HOW BIG IS THE FAMOUS HOLLYWOOD SIGN?

A8 The sign is 450 feet (137 m) long, and each letter is 45 feet (14 m) high. Erected in 1923 as an advertisement for a real estate development, the sign originally said Hollywoodland.

A family from Oklahoma shares tight and temporary quarters in a migrant camp in California.

MGM, Universal, and Warner Bros. opened movie studios in Hollywood and other Southern California locations. They found sunny skies for year-round filming, as well as lots of interesting scenery for backgrounds.

THE DUST BOWL

In the mid-1930s, a drought struck America's Great Plains. The ground was parched. As winds blew, huge dust storms swirled across the plains, creating the conditions called the Dust Bowl. To make things worse, it struck during the **Great Depression**, the worst worldwide economic crisis of the modern era. It began in late 1929 and lasted until 1939. Lines of people waiting for free food could be seen everywhere. Thousands of farm families piled their cars high with household goods and struck out in a vast migration to California.

WORD TO KNOW

Great Depression *an economic downturn in U.S. history (1929 through 1939) when many people lost their jobs and suffered financial difficulties*

For them, California had become the land of their dreams.

Unfortunately, for many people life was no better there. The weather was good, but there were not enough jobs for everyone. They often were unable to find work and lived in deplorable conditions in migrant camps.

A TIME OF WAR

World War II (1939–1945) helped pull the state out of the depression. Industry boomed as California became a center for making aircraft, ships, and weapons. Many military training bases opened in California, too. After Japan attacked the U.S. naval base in Pearl Harbor, Hawaii, on December 7, 1941, the United States entered the war.

Public fear about attacks from outside and within the United States was high. In California, many minorities, including people of Japanese and Mexican descent, sometimes became scapegoats.

Japanese Americans near the West Coast lost their property and liberty when the federal government sent them to **internment camps**. However, from these camps, 33,000 Japanese Americans volunteered to serve in the armed forces. One family sent nine sons to fight for their country. The army's 442nd "Go for Broke" Division was the most decorated unit, with 18,143 awards. Many Japanese Americans served in this unit.

MINI-BIO

NORMAN YOSHIO MINETA: FROM THE CAMPS TO CONGRESS

Norman Yoshio Mineta (1931–) was born in San Jose to Japanese immigrant parents. When he was 10, he and his family were sent to an internment camp near Cody, Wyoming. While he was there, Mineta was a Boy Scout. Alan K. Simpson, a future U.S. senator, visited the camp and introduced the idea of a political career to the boy, and that is exactly the path he followed. As San Jose's mayor (1971–1974), Mineta was the first Asian American mayor of a major U.S. city. He served in the U.S. House of Representatives (1975–1995) and was the U.S. secretary of commerce (2000–2001) and secretary of transportation (2001–2006).

WORD TO KNOW

internment camps *places where large groups of people are confined, usually during a war*

Zoot suits had high-waisted pants and long jackets.

RIOTS AND LAWSUITS

Wartime hysteria targeted people who looked different. In the 1940s in Los Angeles, many young Mexican American men wore zoot suits—high-waisted baggy pants and long suit coats with broad shoulders. This style was easily recognizable, and in the summer of 1943, when a group of angry U.S. servicemen spotted some young men in zoot suits, violence erupted. The soldiers attacked them, and soon the police were also beating and arresting young men in these suits. The Mexican American community responded, and the Zoot Suit Riots continued for a week, highlighting the discrimination and intolerance suffered by Mexican Americans.

There was a different type of fight in Orange County in 1944. To keep Mexican and Mexican American children out of certain public schools, some school districts redrew their boundary lines. When Gonzalo and Felicita Mendez tried to enroll their children in Main Street School, the school district told them their children had to attend a different school. The Mendezes sued the school for segregating their children and won. This case set the stage for the landmark Kansas desegregation case *Brown v. Board of Education*, in which the U.S. Supreme Court ruled that segregation in U.S. public schools was illegal.

SUBURBS AND STRIKES

After the war, many military and defense-industry workers decided to stay in California. Smaller cities soon became bustling urban centers. Wide-open spaces were made into sprawling suburbs, and newly built freeways connected them with the cities. Drive-ins, supermarkets, and shopping malls sprang up everywhere. At the same time, surfers pursued a laid-back, sun-loving lifestyle on California's beaches. In the early 1960s, teenagers all over the nation listened to the Beach Boys sing "Surfin' USA," reinforcing the idea that California was the best place to be in the country.

In agricultural areas, many farms relied on Mexican and Filipino workers. These low-paid migrant laborers moved from one region to another as each crop was ready for harvesting. These workers banded together to form unions. They organized **strikes** and **boycotts**, demanding that growers provide safer working conditions and higher wages.

A STRUGGLE FOR EQUAL RIGHTS

During the 1960s, racial tensions increased. The Watts district of Los Angeles was a working-class African American neighborhood. Residents were angry about police brutality, high unemployment, and underfunded schools. Tempers boiled over in 1965, and riots broke out. Fights and fires raged for six days. Throughout the nation, African Americans and Hispanic Americans fought for fair treatment and civil rights, forming organizations that led protests, held boycotts, and lobbied for legislation.

On March 3, 1991, white police officers pulled over Rodney King, an African American, after a high-speed chase in Los Angeles. Rather than ticket or arrest King for speeding and failing to pull over, four officers assaulted King in the street. A bystander videotaped

WORDS TO KNOW

strikes *organized refusals to work*

boycotts *refusals, usually planned by a group, to buy certain products or use certain services*

MINI-BIO

CÉSAR CHÁVEZ: UNITED FOR A CAUSE

César Chávez's family lost their farm in Arizona during the Depression. They headed to California to work as produce pickers. Chávez (1927–1993) went to 27 schools because his family was always traveling to get work. As a union leader, he led peaceful protest marches. He spoke in fields, at schools, and to government leaders. And the union he cofounded grew stronger. In 1965, it merged with another union to become the United Farm Workers Association, and it continues to champion farmworkers' rights. Today, Chávez's birthday is celebrated as a holiday in California.

King lying on the ground while the officers beat him. King later pressed charges, bringing the four officers to trial. A year later, the officers accused in the case were found not guilty. The verdict enraged the African American community in Los Angeles, people who were already frustrated by poverty and lack of services. It led to riots in the city that claimed the lives of 54 people and cost $1 billion in property damage.

STUDENT VOICES

In the 1960s and 1970s, students across the country were protesting U.S. involvement in the Vietnam War. In many ways, California played a key role in the war.

Vietnam War protesters taking to the streets of San Francisco on April 15, 1967. The march ended with a peace rally.

It was the home of most of the nation's defense contractors—companies that built airplanes, ships, and weapons. It also housed principal military centers from which troops were trained and sent to Vietnam, and it was the scene of antidraft protests. Massive antiwar demonstrations took place on the University of California's Berkeley campus. For young men, one way to make a statement against the war was to burn their draft card. This was a card that male U.S. citizens received from the Selective Service System when they registered for the military draft. Young men who refused to join the military when drafted were called draft resisters. In 1965, there were 380 prosecutions of draft resisters. Three years later, that number had reached 3,305.

This was a time when many people questioned authority. A number of young people, who came to be known as hippies, were urging peace and love. They spoke out against industry, the media, the military, and the government, which they called "The Man," "Big Brother," or "The Establishment." San Francisco's Haight-Ashbury district became a famous hangout for hippies. Their mottoes were heard everywhere—from "Love is all you need" and "All we are saying is give peace a chance" to "Don't trust anyone over 30."

MINI-BIO

TOM BRADLEY: MR. MAYOR

Tom Bradley (1917–1998) was once quoted as saying, "The only thing that will stop you from fulfilling your dreams is you." The first African American mayor of a major U.S. city, Bradley impressed people with the way he handled some big challenges. During his time as Los Angeles's mayor, his city hosted the 1984 Summer Olympic Games. Working to reduce pollution, he pushed to improve public transportation. Bradley also kept the city under control during the 1992 riots sparked by a police incident involving motorist Rodney King.

? **Want to know more?** See www.lausd.k12.ca.us/Tom_Bradley_EL/TBradBio.html

This is a collection of anti–Vietnam War signs from Berkeley. Protesters of the war carried such signs in their marches.

A CHALLENGING OUTLOOK

The last decades of the 20th century saw plenty of growth in California. With the 1970s came the age of the modern computer. Many innovative products were developed right in Silicon Valley.

As California's population and economy grew, so did its pollution. A blanket of smog hung over Los Angeles, caused by heavy traffic. Air pollution affected other cities and even wilderness areas. Coastal waterways were polluted with waste, too. California responded by setting higher emissions standards for cars and limiting construction along the coast.

Natural disasters plagued the state, as well. Earthquakes struck the San Francisco area in 1989 and the Los Angeles area in 1992 and 1994. Throughout the 1990s, Californians suffered droughts, brush fires, floods, and mudslides.

The early 2000s brought power shortages—and a change in power. Electric companies were in financial trouble, and people's electricity bills soared. There were "rolling blackouts" in the summer when electricity was shut off, supposedly because so many people were using their air conditioners. Californians blamed Governor Gray Davis for the power crisis and the state's other financial problems. In 2003, voters elected actor Arnold Schwarzenegger to replace Davis as governor, and reelected him in 2006. His supporters hoped that Schwarzenegger could help with California's problems and set the state on a steady course for the future.

Governor Gray Davis (in blue tie) shown campaigning in the 2003 recall election is accompanied by (from left) Dolores Huerta, Jesse Jackson, and state insurance commissioner John Garamendi.

READ ABOUT

Children take part
in the festivities at
Old Spanish Days
in Santa Barbara.

CHAPTER SIX

PEOPLE

★

AS THE 21ST CENTURY BEGAN, ONE OUT OF EVERY EIGHT AMERICANS—ABOUT 36.5 MILLION PEOPLE—CALLED CALIFORNIA HOME! Although the state ranks third in area, it ranks first in population. What draws new people to California today isn't so different from what has attracted people to California for centuries. It has abundant natural resources and a great climate. So, is California all about sunny beaches, white sand, and surfing? Not exactly. But millions of people have settled along California's Pacific Coast.

Los Angeles highways are several lanes wide and busy with traffic. Some 1.2 million Los Angeles residents drive to work each day.

Big City Life

This chart shows populations of California's biggest cities.

Los Angeles	3,849,378
San Diego	1,256,951
San Jose	929,936
San Francisco	744,041
Long Beach	472,494
Fresno	466,714

Source: U.S. Census Bureau, 2006 estimate

CALIFORNIA, HERE WE COME!

Many people came to California for job opportunities, but most will probably admit they love the roar of the waves, the crunch of the sand, and the feel of ocean breezes.

Most of California's big cities lie along the coast. Los Angeles is the state's largest city. Next in size are San Diego, San Jose, San Francisco, and Long Beach. The two next-largest cities, Fresno and Sacramento—the state's capital—are farther inland.

LIFE IN THE FAST LANE

What's life like in California today? It depends on where you go and who you are. Big-city life in Los Angeles is fast-paced. Around the sprawling city snakes a maze of crowded highways. Along the traffic-jammed downtown streets, people make their way down congested sidewalks on their way to work or the closest coffee shop.

Los Angeles has many unique districts, too. One is Hollywood, known as the capital of the television and movie industries. Another is Beverly Hills, home of the rich and famous. Though city life is hectic, people can escape to the sandy beaches or the hills and valleys nearby.

Life is much more laid back in California's Central Valley. Across its wide-open spaces, lush farmland stretches as far as the eye can see. Population in the valley is growing fast. People move there to escape big-city life or to take farm-related jobs. Still, everyday life is more leisurely, and many cities have the feel of a small community. Dozens of towns hold local harvest festivals. For recreation, residents might go camping or hiking in the surrounding mountains.

California Counties

This map shows the 58 counties in California. Sacramento, the state capital, is indicated with a star.

1. SACRAMENTO
2. CONTRA COSTA
3. SAN JOAQUIN
4. SAN FRANCISCO
5. STANISLAUS

FACES FROM MANY PLACES

Which ethnic group do the majority of Californians belong to? Not any! A majority is more than half, and no group fits that description. Non-Hispanic white people make up the largest ethnic group. Some are descended from American settlers who arrived in the 1800s. Others are descendants of German, Irish, and Italian immigrants. Other newcomers moved to California from countries such as China after World War II.

People QuickFacts

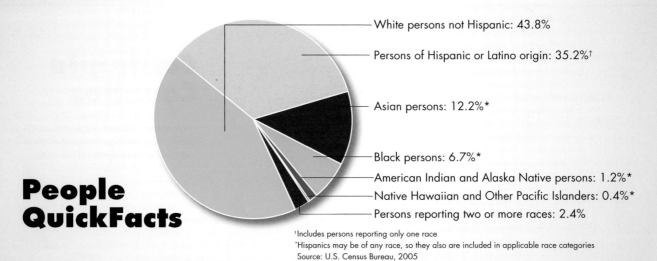

White persons not Hispanic: 43.8%

Persons of Hispanic or Latino origin: 35.2%†

Asian persons: 12.2%*

Black persons: 6.7%*

American Indian and Alaska Native persons: 1.2%*

Native Hawaiian and Other Pacific Islanders: 0.4%*

Persons reporting two or more races: 2.4%

† Includes persons reporting only one race
*Hispanics may be of any race, so they also are included in applicable race categories
Source: U.S. Census Bureau, 2005

Where Californians Live

The colors on this map indicate population density throughout the state. The darker the color, the more people live there.

Population Density
People per square mile

- 1,000 or more
- 250 to 1,000
- 50 to 250
- 10 to 50
- 10 or fewer

Among California's early nonnative residents were people from what is now Mexico. The two places have been linked historically and geographically for hundreds of years. It comes as little surprise that today California has a distinct Hispanic flavor. Hispanic people make up the state's second-largest ethnic group—almost one-third of all Californians. Most of them are Mexican Americans. Others came from Puerto Rico, Cuba, and Central and South American countries.

More people of Asian heritage live in California than in any other state. Chinese Americans make up the state's largest Asian group. San Francisco's Chinatown is the oldest and largest Chinese community in the country. Other Asian Californians have origins in the Philippines, North and South Korea, Vietnam, India, and Japan, among many other countries.

California is also home to more African Americans than any other state. Many arrived to work on railroads after being freed from slavery. Others arrived to

San Francisco's Chinatown, the largest Chinese community in the United States, hosts parades and performances to celebrate Chinese New Year.

About two of every five Californians speak a language other than English at home.

work in shipyards during World War II. Today, like all Californians, they work in all sorts of professions and live in neighborhoods throughout the state.

Native Americans make up 1 percent of California's population. Many of the state's Native people live on dozens of reservations, from the Colorado River Reservation in the south to the Elk Valley Reservation in the north. Reservations are federally recognized land allotments. The groups that inhabit them have limited control over that land, which is really managed by the federal government.

TIME FOR SCHOOL

California's first schools opened in the 1770s. They were mission schools for Native American children. In the 1840s, American settlers began opening their own schools. Beginning in 1867, California children could attend free public elementary schools. But free public high schools weren't available until 1903. Today,

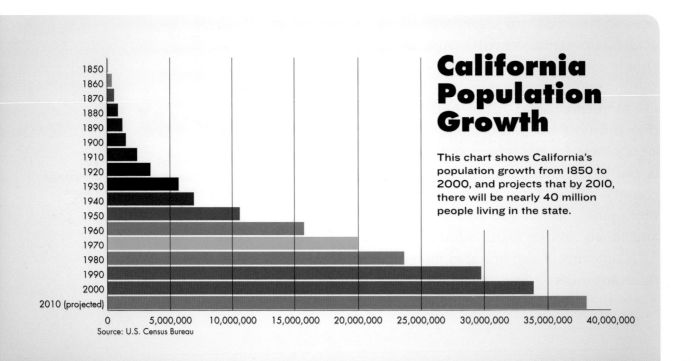

California Population Growth

This chart shows California's population growth from 1850 to 2000, and projects that by 2010, there will be nearly 40 million people living in the state.

Source: U.S. Census Bureau

California has more public school students (approximately 6.3 million in grades K–12) than any other state. Even so, about one out of 12 school-age children, or about 525,000 kids, attend private schools.

Santa Clara College and California Wesleyan College were the first colleges in California. Both of them were private schools opened by religious groups in 1851. Now, they are named Santa Clara University and the University of the Pacific. Today, California's private universities include Stanford University in Palo Alto and the University of Southern California (USC) in Los Angeles.

California State University has more than 20 campuses around the state. The University of California, with ten campuses, is the nation's largest university. Both are state supported.

JAIME ESCALANTE: INNOVATIVE EDUCATOR

Teacher Jaime Escalante (1930–) became famous when he was portrayed by actor Edward James Olmos in the film Stand and Deliver. Escalante taught math in an inner-city Los Angeles high school with a largely Latino population. In 1982, he drew attention when 18 of his Advanced Placement students took and passed the AP calculus exam. But when the Educational Testing Service saw the scores, they thought the students must have cheated, so they threw out the scores. At Escalante's urging, his students took and passed the test a second time.

? Want to know more? See www.nthf.org/inductee/escalante.htm

These Los Angeles students are conducting a chemistry experiment in their classroom.

ALICE WATERS: CREATIVE COOK

Chef Alice Waters (1944–) opened Chez Panisse restaurant in Berkeley in 1971. Her restaurant serves only the best seasonal produce. In 1996, Waters created the Chez Panisse foundation. It supports such educational programs as the Edible Schoolyard, in which gardens are created at public schools where students learn to grow and prepare their own food. At the same time, they build reading skills, learn math and science, and develop better eating habits. Waters received the John Stanford Education Heroes Award in 1999.

? Want to know more?
See www.edibleschoolyard.org

HOW TO TALK LIKE A CALIFORNIAN

Like people everywhere, Californians have their own words for things. What's called a "highway" in many states is a "freeway" in California. More than 15,000 Californians were asked what they call soft drinks. Almost 75 percent said "soda." Only 4 percent said "pop." And what about those long sandwiches on French bread with meat and cheese inside? In much of the country they're "subs" or "hoagies," but in Sacramento, they're "grinders."

HOW TO EAT LIKE A CALIFORNIAN

If there's one thing California has a lot of, it's good, fresh food. Thanks to the state's coastal location, Californians enjoy an abundance of fish and seafood. And thanks to its ideal growing climate, Californians can feast on every kind of fruit and vegetable you might imagine.

Are there dishes that Californians like best? Totally! Look on the next page to see what's on the menu.

MENU

WHAT'S ON THE MENU IN CALIFORNIA?

★ ★ ★

California roll

California Rolls

A California twist on traditional Japanese sushi—avocados, crabmeat, and cucumbers in vinegared rice, wrapped with seaweed.

Monterey Jack cheese

Spanish missionaries in Monterey created this cheese in the 1700s, and in 1882, dairy rancher and businessman David Jacks began making and selling it as "Jacks Cheese." Eventually, it became known as Monterey Jack.

Sourdough Bread

During the gold rush, sourdough bread was an essential food. Now, it's a part of San Francisco culture.

Christmas Tamales

A sweet version of a traditional Mexican food—cornmeal dough filled with fruits, wrapped in corn husks, and steamed.

TRY THIS RECIPE
Avocado Pizza

One thing that California has a lot of is avocados. They are a healthy choice and taste great mixed into things such as guacamole or eaten all by themselves! How about trying one on a pizza? (Be sure to have an adult nearby to help.)

Ingredients:

1 package (13.8 ounces) of refrigerated pizza dough
1 can (12 ounces) of tomato paste
2 pounds small fresh whole tomatoes, sliced
4 ounces low-fat mozzarella cheese, shredded
½ cup Parmesan cheese, grated
½ cup fresh basil, chopped
½ cup green bell pepper, diced
½ cup of any of the following: sliced olives, mushrooms, red onion, or diced red pepper
1 ripe California avocado, pitted, scooped from peel, and sliced

Instructions:

1. Follow directions on the package of pizza dough.
2. Top pizza dough first with tomato paste, then all the other ingredients, except the avocado.
3. Bake in preheated oven at 325°F for 20 minutes.
4. When the pizza is done and has cooled, top it with California avocado slices, making a fun design. You can sprinkle the top with grated Parmesan cheese, if you like.

Avocado pizza

MINI-BIO

GARY SOTO: STORYTELLER

Born in Fresno, Gary Soto (1952—) grew up in a working-class Mexican American neighborhood. His grandparents moved to the United States from Mexico, and his parents worked hard picking grapes, cotton, and oranges in California fields.

A professor of Chicano (Mexican American) studies and English at the University of California-Irvine, he wrote books for young readers, including *Baseball in April and Other Stories, A Fire in My Hands, Taking Sides,* and *Neighborhood Odes.* He enjoys writing poetry, plays, and stories for both young people and adults.

WHAT AN ART!

California's landscape and climate have inspired many artists. Novelist John Steinbeck and photographer Dorothea Lange each created works about the Dust Bowl era. Steinbeck's classic *The Red Pony* tells the story of a boy growing up on a ranch. Nature also fascinated Jack London, whose novel *The Call of the Wild* tells the story of a California dog who has been kidnapped. Samuel Clemens, better known as Mark Twain, wrote funny tales such as "The Celebrated Jumping Frog of Calaveras County."

California writers have compelling stories to tell about the experience of immigrants or people of color. Amy Tan writes about life as a Chinese American in *The Joy Luck Club* (1989).

Young adult books inspired by California include Scott O'Dell's *Island of the Blue Dolphins,* Pam Muñoz Ryan's *Esperanza Rising,* and Laurence Yep's *Dragon Wings.*

A section of *The Great Wall of Los Angeles*, a mural that is a half mile (805 m) long and took five summers to complete

Artist Judith Baca created a project called *The Great Wall of Los Angeles* to celebrate the city's diversity. More than 400 people helped to paint this mural!

SPORTS

What do Olympic figure skater Michelle Kwan, tennis greats Billie Jean King, Pete Sampras, and the Williams sisters, basketball legend Magic Johnson, baseball Hall of Famer Tony Gwynn, and British soccer star David Beckham have in common? California! It is either their birthplace or adopted home.

People may think of surfing when they think of California, but the sport wasn't invented here! It has its roots in Hawaii and Polynesia. By the 1950s, thanks to popular beach-culture movies and music, surfing and California were inseparable.

Today, California's sports teams include the five-time World Series champion Los Angeles Dodgers, the Los Angeles Lakers, winners of 15 NBA titles, and the San Francisco 49ers, who hold five Super Bowl victories. And that's just the pros. To see all the great college teams that play in the state, turn to the sports team list on page 130.

No matter what your sporting interests, in California there's sure to be one for you to watch or play!

MINI-BIO

ELDRICK "TIGER" WOODS: A MIND FOR GOLF

Almost everyone knows the famous face of Eldrick "Tiger" Woods (1975–). He was born and raised in Cypress, went to California public schools, and spent two years at Stanford University.

The story goes that he swung his first club when he was barely able to walk. And he went on the win the U.S. Amateur title three times, something no one else has done. After turning pro in 1996, Woods won the 1997 Masters tournament—the first person of color and the youngest person to win that event. Since then, he has won the other three major tournaments (the U.S. Open, British Open, and PGA Championship) multiple times and is gunning for Jack Nicklaus's record of 18 major titles.

Woods gives back to the community through the Tiger Woods Foundation and the Tiger Woods Learning Center, both based in Southern California.

READ ABOUT

The capitol now houses the executive and legislative branches of state government. It once housed the judicial branch, as well.

CHAPTER SEVEN

GOVERNMENT

★

HIGH SCHOOLER KRISTEN SCHLEICHER WAS SICK AND TIRED OF PUBLIC SCHOOL TEXTBOOKS THAT WERE OFTEN WORN OUT AND OUTDATED. She believed that the books should be reviewed every four years for quality and up-to-date information. In 2000, she submitted this idea to her state lawmakers. She even appeared before them to argue her cause. Within months, Kristen's idea became a state law!

WORDS TO KNOW

constitution *a written document that contains all the governing principles of a state or country*

amendments *changes to a law or legal document*

legislature *the lawmaking body for a state or country*

California amended its constitution more than 460 times during the 20th century.

CALIFORNIA CONSTITUTION

In the fall of 1849, a group of 48 people met for six weeks in Monterey to draft California's first **constitution**. By 1877, citizens' thoughts about politics had changed and they were worried about economic depression. They voted to hold a meeting to revise the constitution to address those problems. The voters adopted a new constitution in 1879. Since then, they have created **amendments** many times.

THE LEGISLATIVE BRANCH

A **legislature's** job is to pass state laws. California's is composed of two branches, the state Senate and the state Assembly. Both meet in the state capitol. That's the building you see pictured below. It is in Sacramento, the capital city.

Californians also elect people to represent them in the two houses of the U.S. Congress. Like other states, California elects two U.S. senators. It also elects 53 U.S. representatives. That's more representatives than any other state gets. Why so many? Because the number of U.S. representatives is determined by population—and California has the nation's highest population.

Capitol Facts

Here are some fascinating facts about California's state capitol.

Exterior height	220 feet (67 m)
Height of interior dome	120 feet (37 m)
Number of stories high	4*
Length	320 feet (98 m)*
Width	164 feet (50 m)*
Surrounding park	40 acres (16 ha)
Location	10th Street between L and N Streets, Sacramento
Construction dates	1860–1874*
Cost of construction	$245 million

*Excludes annex added in 1952

The capitol in Sacramento

Capital City

This map shows places of
interest in Sacramento,
California's capital city.

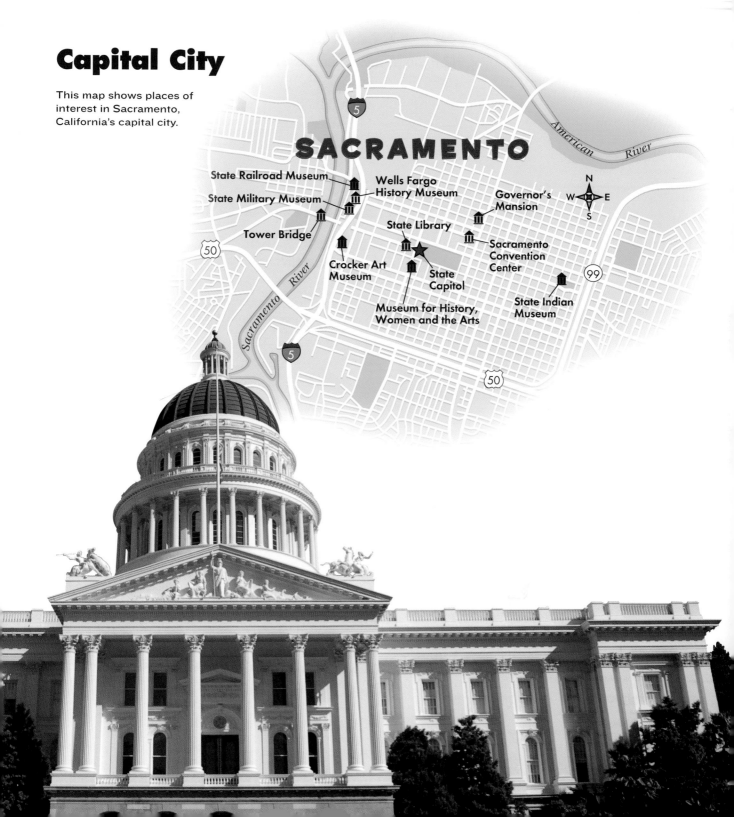

SACRAMENTO

American River

State Railroad Museum

State Military Museum

Tower Bridge

Wells Fargo
History Museum

Crocker Art
Museum

State Library

State
Capitol

Museum for History,
Women and the Arts

Governor's
Mansion

Sacramento
Convention
Center

State Indian
Museum

Sacramento River

N W E S

THE EXECUTIVE BRANCH

The job of the executive branch is to carry out state laws. California's governor is the chief executive, or head of the executive branch. His or her office is in the state capitol. Voters elect the governor to a four-year term. In California, a governor can serve only two terms in a row.

California's State Government

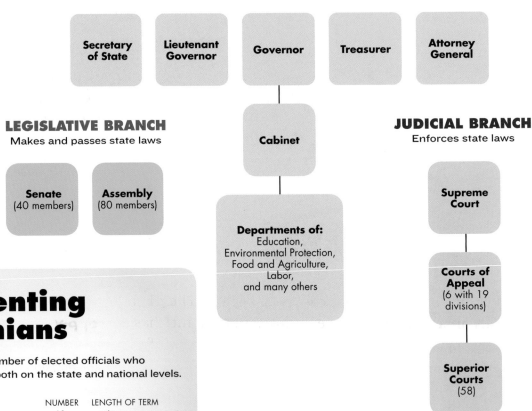

EXECUTIVE BRANCH
Carries out state laws

Secretary of State

Lieutenant Governor

Governor

Treasurer

Attorney General

Cabinet

Departments of:
Education,
Environmental Protection,
Food and Agriculture,
Labor,
and many others

LEGISLATIVE BRANCH
Makes and passes state laws

Senate (40 members)

Assembly (80 members)

JUDICIAL BRANCH
Enforces state laws

Supreme Court

Courts of Appeal (6 with 19 divisions)

Superior Courts (58)

Representing Californians

This list shows the number of elected officials who represent California, both on the state and national levels.

OFFICE	NUMBER	LENGTH OF TERM
State senator	40	4 years
State assembly member	80	2 years
U.S. senator	2	6 years
U.S. representative	53	2 years
Presidential electors	55	—

Want to know more? See: http://capitolmuseum. ca.gov/english/citizens/government/index.html

Carrying out the laws is a massive job, so voters elect several other executive officers to take charge of special areas. They include the lieutenant governor, secretary of state, attorney general, treasurer, controller, insurance commissioner, and superintendent of public instruction.

THE JUDICIAL BRANCH

The judicial branch of government is made up of California's court system. The judges who serve on the courts are responsible for deciding whether someone has broken the law. Judges listen to cases in courts. They hear the evidence for and against someone, and they study what the law says. That's how they make their decisions.

California has three levels of courts. The highest court is the state supreme court. It has a chief justice, or judge, and six associate justices. Beneath the supreme court are several district courts of appeal. They hear cases on **appeal** from lower courts. Each county has a superior, or trial, court. These courts hold most of the state's major trials.

LOCAL RULE

Besides the state government, California has county and city governments. Most of California's 58 counties elect a five-member board of supervisors. They also

WORD TO KNOW

appeal *a legal proceeding in which a court is asked to change the decision of a lower court*

elect officers such as county assessor, auditor, clerk, coroner, district attorney, sheriff, school superintendent, and treasurer.

Most of the cities elect a city manager and a city council to govern them. Some elect a mayor and a city council. As of 2005, California had 478 **incorporated** cities. Among those, 108 are chartered cities. What is a chartered city? It's a city that has home rule. That is, it has drawn up its own **charter**. This gives the city a lot of control over local affairs. Any city with at least 3,500 residents can choose to adopt home rule.

WORDS TO KNOW

incorporated *recognized as a self-governing entity*

charter *a basic set of rules*

CALIFORNIANS IN THE WHITE HOUSE

Richard Milhous Nixon (1913–1994) was the 37th U.S. president (1969–1974). He resigned during the Watergate scandal, becoming the only U.S. president to resign his office. Nixon was born in Yorba Linda.

Ronald Wilson Reagan (1911–2004) was the 40th U.S. president (1981–1989). Born in Illinois, he moved to California and became a movie actor. He was California's governor from 1967 to 1975.

MINI-BIO

MADAME SPEAKER

Nancy Pelosi (1940–) has represented California's Eighth District in the U.S. House of Representatives since 1987. The district includes most of the city of San Francisco. In fall 2002, she was elected Democratic (minority) Leader of the House of Representatives. She is the first woman in U.S. history to lead a major party in the U.S. Congress. When the Democrats took control of the House following the 2006 election, Pelosi became the first woman Speaker of the U.S. House of Representatives.

 Want to know more? See www.house.gov/pelosi

POWER TO THE PEOPLE!

Have you ever been mad about something and declared, "There ought to be a law. . . ."? If you live in California, you can make that law happen.

California has several ways for citizens to take the law into their own hands. One is by an initiative. This gives people the power to propose new laws. They can also propose amendments, or changes to the state constitution.

Another powerful tool is the referendum. This allows citizens to keep a new law from taking effect. Unlike in other states, California citizens also have a way to remove public officials they're not pleased with. It's called a recall. Californians used the recall to remove Governor Gray Davis from office in 2003.

WACKY LAWS

California has some pretty wacky laws. Though the laws below are rarely, if ever, enforced, they are still on the books.

- Throughout the state, no vehicle without a driver may exceed 60 miles per hour (97 kph).
- People in Blythe may not wear cowboy boots unless they own at least two cows.
- No one in Los Angeles may lick a toad.
- In Cathedral City, it is illegal to bring a dog to school.
- In Eureka, a man with a moustache may not kiss a woman.

At election time, Californians often have referendums to consider. Signs like these try to tell the people how to cast their votes.

Save Our Community From

NO on 4A

QUAL

YES ON 04-A MEASURE
Good News for Inglewood!

State Flag

California's state flag is called the Bear Flag. It features a red star and a grizzly bear on a white background. Underneath are the words *California Republic* and a red band. Grizzlies were common in the wilds of California. The star is an imitation of the "lone star" of the Texas flag. William Todd made the first Bear Flag on a piece of unbleached cotton cloth. In the Bear Flag Revolt of June 14, 1846, settlers took over the Mexican headquarters at Sonoma. They raised the Bear Flag and declared California an independent republic. After statehood in 1850, the U.S. stars and stripes flew over California. The Bear Flag was declared the state flag in 1911.

State Seal

The California state seal depicts the ancient Roman goddess of wisdom, Minerva. At her feet is a grizzly bear, an animal common in the state at the time of the gold rush. In the background is the Sacramento River, with a miner digging for gold along its banks. Ships on the river stand for California's trade. Also in the background are the mountains of the Sierra Nevada. At the top is the word *Eureka*, which is Greek for "I have found it!"

94

California farms grow an array of vegetables and they are the top producer of many crops in the United States.

CHAPTER EIGHT

ECONOMY

★

ONLY ABOUT 3 PERCENT OF ITS LABOR FORCE WORK ON FARMS, YET CALIFORNIA IS THE NATION'S TOP AGRICULTURAL STATE. It grows more food and exports more farm products than any other state.

Farmland covers approximately one-third of California's total land area. Crops grow on one-third of that land, while the rest is grazing land for cattle, sheep, and other livestock. Farms are often called ranches, whether they raise crops or animals.

This 4-H member is preparing to show his calf at the Los Angeles County Fair in Pomona. All kinds of farm animals are judged at California county fairs.

LIFE ON A CALIFORNIA FARM

What do you do when you get home from school? Do you play on the computer, do your homework, practice soccer, or watch TV? After-school life is a bit different for Gretchen, Holly, and Chester. They help raise sheep on their family's farm in Woodland. The kids feed and clean the sheep. They also help with shearing, or shaving off, the sheep's wool.

Sheep farming is hard work, but the kids don't mind. "It's good training for the future," says Holly. "We can tackle problems that a lot of other kids might not be able to."

Young people help out on many of California's farms. The state has about 77,000 farms, and most of them are family owned. Farm kids look forward to their county fairs. They bring animals they've raised and enter them in competitions. All their hard work pays off when they walk away with a prize!

THE NATION'S SALAD BOWL

Almonds, apricots, asparagus, avocados, bell peppers, boysenberries, broccoli, cantaloupes, carrots, cauliflower, celery, garlic, grapes, lettuce, milk, olives, onions, plums, raspberries, spinach, strawberries, walnuts—the list of California's top crops is impressive. Suppose you're making a big bowl of salad. What would you put in it? Most likely you would begin with some lettuce, then add some or many of the items listed above (well, probably not the milk). California is the top U.S. producer of all those ingredients. In fact, the state produces more than half of all the fruits, nuts, and vegetables sold in the whole country.

California's Central Valley is often called "the nation's salad bowl." It's the state's richest farming region. The valley's southern area, the San Joaquin Valley, is the most productive of all. And Fresno County is the most productive county. It grows more farm products than 22 of the U.S. states!

Milk is the state's leading farm product. California farmers raise dairy and beef cattle, sheep, hogs, turkeys, and chickens.

Grapes are the state's number-two product. They're sold fresh or made into wine, grape juice, and raisins. Other top fruits are lemons, kiwifruits, peaches, and strawberries. Nut crops include almonds and walnuts. Nursery products are valuable, too. They include cut flowers, potted plants, and decorative trees.

Major Agricultural and Mining Products

This map shows where California's major agricultural and mining products come from. See a yellow brick? That means gold is found there.

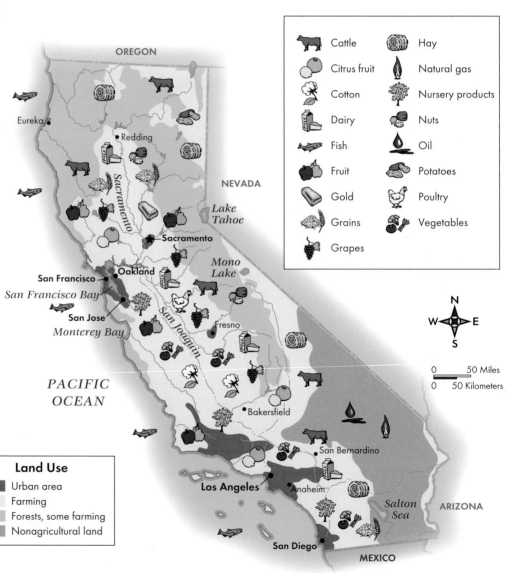

The Apple empire began in a small California garage. Steve Jobs and Steve Wozniak created a company that went on to produce Macintosh computers, iPods (like those above), and iPhones.

FACTORY GOODS

Where do California's crops go? Some go to farmers' markets and grocery stores. Others go to food-processing plants. There they might be dried, cut up, canned, baked, bottled, or frozen.

Computers and electronic equipment are the state's top factory goods, though. Most of them are made in the Santa Clara Valley—also known as Silicon Valley. It's the nation's leading area for manufacturing computer equipment. Intel, Hewlett-Packard, and hundreds of other computer and electronics companies are based there. Their factories make computers, computer chips, telephones, and other communications equipment.

Chemical products are important factory goods, too. They include medicines, cleansers, and paint. California also makes transportation equipment such as aircraft, missiles, spacecraft, ships, and cars.

The Jelly Belly factory in Fairfield makes more than 14 billion jelly beans a year. String all of them together, and they'd circle Earth more than seven times!

THE HIGH-TECH EXPLOSION

It's a common scene—two guys tinkering around with gadgets in a garage. But in 1976, the two guys in a Los Altos garage were Steve Wozniak and Steve Jobs. And their gadgets turned out to be the first Apple computers!

Apple became just one of California's high-tech companies. During the 1970s, the state became a world leader in producing computers, video games, and other electronics.

Most of the computer-related industries opened in the Santa Clara Valley, between Palo Alto and San Jose. This area was dubbed Silicon Valley, after the material used in making computer chips. Eventually, thousands of high-tech companies made their headquarters in Silicon Valley or nearby. They range from the company that developed the Internet search engine Google to the animation studio Pixar.

TOP PRODUCTS

Agriculture
Milk, grapes, nursery products

Manufacturing
Computer and electronic equipment, food products, chemicals

Mining
Petroleum (oil), sand and gravel, boron

Fishing
Crabs, squid, salmon

In California, there are many oil refineries near San Francisco Bay and Los Angeles. Oil refineries produce petroleum products such as unleaded gasoline, diesel, and jet fuel.

MINING

What is California's top mining product? If you lived in the 1850s, you'd say "Gold!" That was before there were cars that needed fuel. California's is the fourth—largest producer of petroleum, or oil, in the United States. No other state produces more nonfuel minerals, though. California leads the nation in mining construction minerals such as sand and gravel.

California is the only state that produces boron. It's used in making eyedrops, bug killers, cleansers, and many other substances. Diatomite is another important mineral. It's a soft rock mostly composed of tiny dead sea animals called diatoms. Diatomite is used in a variety of products, from swimming pool filters to toothpaste.

The gold rush may be over, but California is still a leading U.S. producer of gold. Other California minerals include silver, gemstones, clay, soda ash, salt, copper, feldspar, titanium, and magnesium.

CONSERVATION AND ALTERNATIVE ENERGY

Sunshine and wind are also resources in California. The state offers incentives to homeowners and businesses to switch to solar energy, and California has more than 13,000 wind turbines that generate energy for electricity. The turbines are mainly concentrated in three areas: Altamont Pass, Tehachapi, and San Gorgonio.

Natural freshwater sources are rare in much of California, so water conservation is especially important for managing this resource.

FISHING

Do you like seafood? Californians sure do. And it's no wonder. Just look at that long California coastline. Fishing boats haul in tons of fish and shellfish every day.

For wind turbines to work efficiently, winds need to blow at least 12 miles per hour (19 kph).

What Do Californians Do?

This color-coded chart shows what industries Californians work in.

18.6% Educational services, and health care, and social assistance, 2,982,972

11.8% Professional, scientific, and management, and administrative and waste management services, 1,889,224

11.2% Manufacturing, 1,793,833

11.2% Retail trade, 1,791,422

8.7% Arts, entertainment, and recreation, and accommodation, and food services, 1,395,401

8.0% Construction, 1,257,180

7.5% Finance and insurance, and real estate and rental and leasing, 1,215,715

5.1% Other services, except public administration, 817,105

4.6% Transportation and warehousing, and utilities, 730,274

4.5% Public administration, 723,223

4.0% Wholesale trade, 636,007

2.9% Information, 479,011

1.8% Agriculture, forestry, fishing and hunting, and mining, 297,177

Source: U.S. Census Bureau, 2005 estimate

A commercial fisher with a bucket of fresh crabs on the dock of the Santa Barbara harbor

Crabs are the top catch, and Dungeness crabs are the most valuable. Crabbers head out to sea in their boats and drop crab pots, which are metal cages, along their route. A few days later, they come back and haul up the pots full of crabs.

Squid is the number-two catch, followed by salmon. California fishers also catch lobsters, shrimp, swordfish, sardines, and many other species. Aquaculture, or fish farming, is a growing industry, too. California's fish farms raise salmon, trout, and other popular fish.

AT YOUR SERVICE

In the 1850s, California's leading industry was mining. Later, agriculture took over. By 1900, manufacturing took the lead. Today, services hold the top spot. California's service industries earn more income than any other industry in the state. Tourism accounts for much of this income. Tourists spend money in theme parks, campsites, restaurants, hotels, and museums. Even grocery stores are service businesses. You may buy a tomato there. But the store provides the service of getting it from the farm to the grocery-store display.

California's hospitals, banks, laundries, and movie studios are service companies. So are firms specializing in law, engineering, and computer software design. Other service companies do medical research, sell houses, or repair cars. Even the government is a service industry. It provides a range of services, from public schools to drivers' licenses. As you can see, Californians are good at saying, "How may I serve you?"

MINI-BIO

103

EARVIN "MAGIC" JOHNSON: BEYOND BASKETBALL

One of the most exciting players on a basketball court, Earvin "Magic" Johnson (1959–) was born in East Lansing, Michigan. Johnson played 13 seasons with the Los Angeles Lakers, where he won five NBA championships and was named to the NBA all-star team 12 times.

After he retired, Johnson turned his attention to business ventures. Magic Johnson Enterprises partners with other corporations, such as Starbucks, Washington Mutual Bank, and Burger King, throughout the country. And the joint venture with 24 Hour Fitness boasts ten facilities in California.

He also created the Magic Johnson Foundation, a nonprofit organization that supports the health and education of young people. It is based in Southern California.

 Want to know more? See www.magicjohnson.org

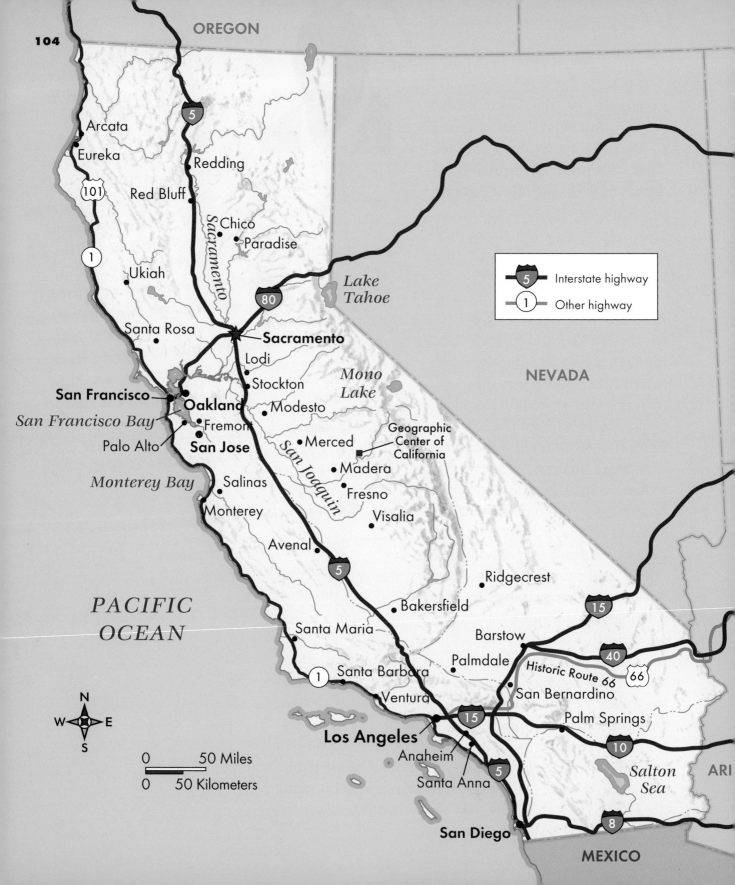

OREGON

104

Arcata

Eureka

101

Redding

Red Bluff

Sacramento

Chico

Paradise

Ukiah

Lake Tahoe

Santa Rosa

5	Interstate highway
1	Other highway

80

Sacramento

Lodi

Stockton

Mono Lake

NEVADA

San Francisco

Oakland

Modesto

San Francisco Bay

Fremont

San Joaquin

Palo Alto

San Jose

Merced

Geographic Center of California

Monterey Bay

Salinas

Madera

Monterey

Fresno

Visalia

Avenal

Ridgecrest

PACIFIC OCEAN

5

Bakersfield

15

Santa Maria

Barstow

Palmdale

40

Historic Route 66

66

N
W   E
S

Santa Barbara

1

San Bernardino

Ventura

Palm Springs

15

10

0   50 Miles

0   50 Kilometers

Los Angeles

Anaheim

Salton Sea

ARI

Santa Anna

5

MEXICO

San Diego

8

TRAVEL GUIDE

TRAVEL GUIDE

★

READY TO DO SOME SIGHTSEEING? From Disneyland to the La Brea Tar Pits, from spectacular surf to SeaWorld, this travel guide will take you to dozens of destinations in California. Take a look and you will see why more than 375 million tourists visit California every year—making it the number-one travel destination in the United States!

← Follow along with this travel map. We'll begin in Eureka and travel all the way down to San Diego!

NORTH COAST

THINGS TO DO: See the world's tallest trees, visit a beautiful seaport, and go for a boat ride.

Eureka

★ **Redwood National Forest:** Hike through this incredible forest and marvel at the world's tallest trees. In fact, you'll find Hyperion here. It's the world's tallest tree and measures 379 feet (116 m) tall. More than 112,000 acres (45,300 ha) are home to redwoods that can live for thousands of years.

Redwood National Forest

Sonoma

★ **Bear Flag Monument:** Sonoma is known as the birthplace of American California. This is where the Bear Flag Revolt took place and a Bear Flag was first raised. Stop by and see the monument in Sonoma Plaza.

SHASTA CASCADE

THINGS TO DO: Take a bike ride, go camping, cross an incredible bridge, and see the world's largest yo-yo.

Redding

★ **Shasta Lake:** Spend a night or two camping along the shores of this stunning lake. The backdrop of majestic peaks will take your breath away.

★ **Turtle Bay Exploration Park:** Visit the butterfly house—an enclosed garden with hundreds of species of butterflies—or explore a Wintu bark house and learn about this Native American culture. And walk across the incredible Sundial Bridge, a pedestrian walkway over the Sacramento River. Want to know more? See www.turtlebay.org

Chico

★ **National Yo-Yo Museum:** This museum boasts the Duncan family collection of yo-yos from the 1920s to

the 1950s, as well as the world's largest yo-yo, which is 50 inches (127 cm) high, weighs 250 pounds (113 kilograms), and has 75 feet (23 m) of string!

BAY AREA
THINGS TO DO:
Ride a cable car, eat authentic Chinese food and explore ancient Egypt.

San Francisco

★ **Alcatraz Island:** Situated in the San Francisco Bay, Alcatraz was established as a military prison in 1850, and became a federal prison in 1933. Such famous bad guys as Al Capone and Franklin Stroud (the Birdman of Alcatraz) were held there. In 1963, the land became a national recreation area, and it's now open for tours.

★ **Fisherman's Wharf:** Hear the sea lions bark as they sun themselves on the piers. Pick up a bag of saltwater taffy, taste some seafood, or watch fish merchants selling the catch of the day.

★ **Cable Car Museum:** Located on Mason Street, this museum has antique cable cars dating back to the 1870s—be sure to ride a cable car while you're in town!

★ **The Presidio:** Once a Spanish military base, it's now a national park with forests, beaches, hiking trails, and historic buildings.

★ **Lombard Street:** It's called "the crookedest street in the world" because of its zigzag turns. The street begins at the Presidio and ends at the Embarcadero on the waterway and is best known for its eight sharp turns between Hyde and Leavenworth streets.

★ **Golden Gate Park:** Wander along its winding footpaths and feel as if you're deep in a forest. The park is home to more than 1 million trees, and about 75,000 people visit each weekend.

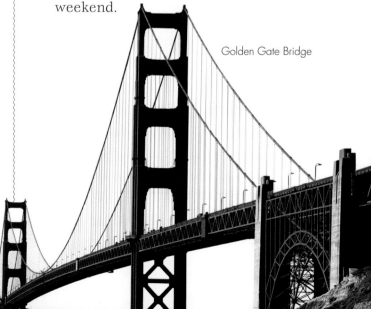

Golden Gate Bridge

★ **Chinatown:** Established in the 1850s, it's the oldest and biggest Chinatown in North America. Sample traditional Chinese foods and be sure to visit the Golden Gate Fortune Cookie Factory.

★ **AT&T Park:** Home of the San Francisco Giants major league baseball team, this ballpark features an inspiring 9-foot (2.7-m) statue of the "Say Hey Kid," the great Willie Mays.

Willie Mays statue at AT&T Park

Oakland

★ **Chabot Space & Science Center:** This amazing facility is home to observatories that bring outer space to you! One of its telescopes allows a 180-degree view of the sky. And the 240-seat planetarium has an impressive 70-foot (21-m) dome.

San Jose

★ **Rosicrucian Egyptian Museum & Planetarium:** This museum houses the largest collection of Egyptian artifacts on exhibit in the United States.

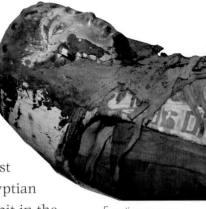

Egyptian mummy

Santa Cruz

★ **Beach Boardwalk:** This is California's oldest amusement park, and it is home to the 1924 Giant Dipper roller coaster and the 1911 Looff Carousel.

GOLD COUNTRY

THINGS TO DO: Tour through the state capitol, go fly-fishing in the North Yuba River, and go kayaking down the American River near Auburn.

Sacramento

★ **California State Capitol:** Take a walk through the beautifully landscaped Capitol Park, which leads to the state capitol. Sit in on a senate session or perhaps even visit with the governor.

- ★ **Old Sacramento:** Ever wondered about life during the gold rush? Tour Old Sacramento and see a show at the historic Eagle Theater, take a ride on a horse-drawn carriage or an antique riverboat, and walk through the historic streets.
- ★ **Towe Auto Museum:** Tour fascinating exhibits featuring some of the oldest cars, including the Ford Model T. See the history of automobile design from its beginnings to the present.
- ★ **Sacramento Zoo:** You'll meet a variety of animals at this 14.3-acre (5.8-ha) zoo, from chimpanzees and red pandas to the thick-billed parrot and the rainbow boa!

SEE IT HERE!

PAN FOR GOLD

Sutter's Mill, where James Marshall found gold, is now part of the Marshall Gold Discovery State Historic Park in Coloma. There, you'll learn all about the gold rush. You'll also see sawmill demonstrations and even learn how to pan for gold. Then, you can head on down to the American River and try it yourself! Good luck!

Sierra City

- ★ **North Yuba River:** This river offers some of the best fly-fishing in the country. And its 18 miles (29 km) of white water beckon the experienced kayaker in the spring.

Auburn

- ★ **Auburn Iron Works:** Here you can see one of the oldest blacksmith shops in the state—it has been in operation for more than 100 years!
- ★ **Old Town Firehouse:** Established in 1891, and still active, the Old Town Firehouse is one of the oldest volunteer firefighting organizations in the West. The firehouse bell chimes at 8 A.M., noon, and 5 P.M.!

CENTRAL VALLEY

THINGS TO DO: Drive through lush, fertile California farmland; visit with exotic zoo animals; and ride the Pixie Express train!

Fresno

- ★ **Fresno Metropolitan Museum of Art and Science:** Exhibits at the Met include more than 3,000 works of art and artifacts drawn from several cultures spanning more than 400 years!

★ **Legion of Valor Veterans Museum:** Stop by the Legion of Valor Veterans Museum, where you can see numerous framed citations, photographs, and exhibits that tell the story of American military history as experienced by individual soldiers, sailors, and pilots!

Stockton

★ **Haggin Museum:** This museum's art collection features works by noted 19th-century painters such as Albert Bierstadt, Rosa Bonheur, and William-Adolphe Bouguereau, as well as many other American and European artists.

SEE IT HERE!

HAVE AN AGVENTURE

How does food get from the farm to your table? You'll find out at AgVentures! in Tulare. It's a hands-on agricultural museum. There, you'll hop on a tractor and take a virtual tour of a farm. See how milk is turned into cheese and ice cream. You can even try your hand at milking a cow!

HIGH SIERRA

THINGS TO DO: Swim or ski in Lake Tahoe, or hike and climb in the awe-inspiring mountain ranges of eastern California.

Yosemite Village

★ **Yosemite National Park:** One of the most spectacular geological gems in the nation! The 750,000-acre (303,500-ha) park is a place of cascading waterfalls, amazing rock formations, magnificent vistas, and towering sequoias.

Coyote in Yosemite National Park

Tahoe City

★ **Lake Tahoe:** Visit in summer for great swimming and boating. Come back in winter for awesome skiing and snowboarding. Along the Truckee River you can fly-fish, raft, and hike.

CENTRAL COAST

THINGS TO DO: Drive along Highway 1 for breathtaking coastline views, visit Hearst Castle, kayak along the central coast of California, and find yourself in teddy bear heaven!

San Simeon

★ **Hearst Castle:** Picture yourself living in this former home of newspaper magnate William Randolph Hearst, with its tapestries, Spanish and Italian art, and Egyptian statues! What would you do with 115 rooms, 38 bedrooms, and 30 fireplaces?

Monterey

★ **The Monterey Museum of the American Indian:** Located upstairs in the Pacific House of Monterey, the museum displays hand-woven baskets, pottery, and other Native American artifacts.

★ **Monterey Bay Aquarium:** Stop by in person or check out the aquarium's Web site at http://www.mbayaq.org. Through live Web cams you can see penguins in the Splash Zone or sea turtles in the open ocean.

Monterey Bay Aquarium

Santa Barbara

★ **Old Mission Santa Barbara:** More than 200 years after its founding, the mission remains the chief cultural and historic landmark in the city of Santa Barbara!

★ **Susan Quinlan Doll and Teddy Bear Museum and Library:** Three galleries "stuffed" with 3,000 dolls and teddy bears, from antique to modern.

DESERT

THINGS TO DO: Enjoy scenic canyon views from an aerial tramway, tour the rocky countryside, or see a real meteorite!

Palm Springs

★ **Palm Springs Aerial Tramway:** Take the 10-minute ride aboard the world's largest rotating tramcar, and experience a breathtaking journey up the sheer cliffs of Chino Canyon.

Joshua Tree

★ **Palm Springs Air Museum:** This expansive collection of aircraft features propeller-driven World War II aircraft in flying condition.

★ **Joshua Tree National Park:** Tour the Mojave and Lower Colorado deserts where they join in this national park. Camp, hike, or ride horseback in this other-worldly landscape.

Barstow

★ **Desert Discovery Center:** At the Desert Discovery Center, you can view the Old Woman Springs Meteorite, the second-largest space rock ever found in the United States.

SEE IT HERE!
THE WORLD'S LARGEST SHOE
You may do a double take when you see this wacky sight in Bakersfield. It's a shoe repair shop that was built in 1947—in the shape of a shoe. It measures 25 feet (7.6 m) high, 32 feet (9.8 m) long, and is equal to a size 678.

LOS ANGELES
THINGS TO DO: Take a stroll down the Walk of Fame, shop on Rodeo Drive, or go see a show with the family at the world-famous Kodak Theatre!

★ **California African American Museum:** On exhibit are artifacts from West Africa that represent the art, history, and culture of the region. You'll learn about African Americans' southern legacy, the Great Migration west, and the many contributions that African Americans made in opening the western frontier.

Hollywood

★ **Ripley's Believe It Or Not! Museum:** Interested in the odd, abnormal, or flat-out twisted? At Ripley's Believe It Or Not! Museum you can see a collection of nearly 300 unusual and strange exhibits from all over the world!

Entrance to Ripley's Believe It or Not!

SEE IT HERE!

LA BREA TAR PITS

In the middle of the Miracle Mile district in Los Angeles are the La Brea Tar Pits.

Thousands of years ago, the pits were much as they are today: sticky, hot, and bubbling. Small mammals, birds, and insects were trapped in the pits. Larger animals would step in and find their feet immediately sinking several inches below the surface. Many died there or were gobbled up by a passing predator. Experts think that at least ten animals were caught every 30 years.

For the last 100 years, researchers have been removing and studying ancient bones from these pits. The bones are protected by the asphalt, a tarlike substance, which preserves them.

★ **Universal Studios Hollywood:** In the mood for a theme park and the movies? Universal Studios Hollywood combines both! Rides take you through some of your favorite movies, from *Jaws* and *King Kong* to *Back to the Future.* Take a tour through the back lots of the studios, where some of today's blockbuster hits are filmed.

★ **Grauman's Chinese Theatre:** Since its gala opening in May 1927, millions of movie fans and visitors to Hollywood have been drawn to this theater. They come to be entertained and enthralled by the legendary theater, home to the Forecourt of Stars, where you can try to fit your hands and feet into the concrete impressions made by Hollywood's most famous actors.

Pasadena

★ **Rose Bowl Stadium:** The location of the New Year's Tournament of Roses football game, the stadium has also earned its world-class reputation by hosting five NFL Super Bowl games and lots of other memorable events over its 80-year history.

INLAND EMPIRE

THINGS TO DO: Whether you like baseball, shopping, swimming, or golfing, there is plenty to do in the Inland Empire region.

San Bernardino

★ **California Route 66 Museum:** Here you'll find exhibits of the contemporary artwork of the "Main Street of America." The museum boasts a collection of historic Route 66 signs, postcards, and vintage cars!

Riverside

★ **March Field Air Museum:** This museum features exhibits depicting the history of March Air Force Base, 53 vintage aircraft, and memorabilia dating from World War I to the present.

ORANGE COUNTY

THINGS TO DO: Enjoy world-class shopping, amusement parks, a major league baseball game, or learn how to scuba dive or surf!

Anaheim

★ **Anaheim Angels:** Take in a major league baseball game at Angels Stadium of Anaheim, home to the Anaheim Angels!

★ **Disneyland Park:** From Main Street U.S.A. to Mickey's Toontown, this land of the Magic Kingdom will bring fairy tales to life.

★ **Disneyland's California Adventure Park:** Free-fall into excitement and thrills on the Twilight Zone Tower of Terror, or step into the world of Disney animation and be part of many interactive animation shows.

MINI-BIO

WALT DISNEY: MAGICAL MAN

Everybody knows the mouse ears and the name of the man who created them—Walt Disney (1901–1966). Disney was a pioneer in motion-picture animation. His first Mickey Mouse cartoons appeared in 1928. His first feature-length films were Snow White (1937; the first-ever feature-length animated film), Pinocchio (1938), and Bambi (1942). In 1955, he opened Disneyland, the world's first theme park, in Anaheim. Disney World, in Orlando, Florida, opened in 1971. Today, the Walt Disney Company includes 11 theme parks, 39 hotels, eight film studios, six record labels, and 11 cable television networks.

Laguna Beach

★ **Glenn E. Vedder Ecological Reserve Laguna Beach Underwater Park and Tide Pools:** Scuba divers and snorkelers, this is the place for you! A reserve for marine life, plants, game fish, shells, and rocks. A diver's paradise.

SAN DIEGO

THINGS TO DO: Visit Shamu, the star of SeaWorld, visit world-famous museums, or enjoy a stroll along San Diego's beautiful coastline!

San Diego

★ **The San Diego Firehouse Museum:** Here you'll learn about the importance of firefighting in San Diego. See exhibits of firefighting equipment from the 1800s, fire trucks from the early 1900s, and a somber 9/11 tribute and memorial.

★ **Maritime Museum of San Diego:** This museum features one of the world's finest collections of historic ships. It includes the world's oldest active ship, *Star of India*, H.M.S. *Surprise* from the Academy Award–winning film *Master and Commander*, the 1898 steam ferry *Berkeley*, the 1904 steam yacht *Medea*, and a B-39 Soviet-era submarine.

★ **SeaWorld San Diego:** You'll see the black and white of penguins and killer whales, and all colors in between, at SeaWorld. Experience the thrills of Journey to Atlantis and the playful fun of Shamu's Happy Harbor.

★ **Legoland California:** Enjoy more than 50 thrill rides, become a pirate on a galleon ship, pretend you're a firefighter, or charge into a tournament as a brave knight. All in a day's fun at Legoland!

★ **San Diego Zoo:** What will you find at the San Diego Zoo? Giant pandas living in a natural environment of bamboo. Rhinos, giraffes, gazelles, zebras, ostriches, and creatures too numerous to list, on the Journey into Africa Tour. The center for the Conservation and Research for Endangered Species, and much, much more

★ **San Diego de Alcalá:** Mission San Diego is the oldest mission in California, and the first link in the "chain" of missions that stretches 650 miles (1,046 km) along the El Camino Real, or King's Highway.

Killer whale at SeaWorld San Diego

WRITING PROJECTS

Check out these ideas for creating great PowerPoint presentations and writing you-are-there editorials. Or learn about the state quarter and design your own.

118

ART PROJECTS 119

Make a diorama from two different time periods, illustrate the state song, or build a California mission.

TIMELINE

122

What happened when? This timeline highlights important events in the state's history—and shows what was happening throughout the United States at the same time.

FAST FACTS 126

Use this section to find fascinating facts about state symbols, land area and population statistics, weather, sports teams, and much more.

GLOSSARY 125

Remember the Words to Know from the chapters in this book? They're all collected here.

SCIENCE, TECHNOLOGY, & MATH PROJECTS

Create earthquake charts, map bird migrations, and research important inventors and scientists from the state.

120

PRIMARY VS. SECONDARY SOURCES

121

So what are primary and secondary sources and what's the diff? This section explains all that and where you can find them.

BIOGRAPHICAL DICTIONARY

133

This at-a-glance guide highlights some of the state's most important and influential people. Visit this section and read up about their contributions to the state, the country, and the world.

RESOURCES

Books, Web sites, DVDs, and more. Take a look at these additional sources for information about the state.

137

WRITING PROJECTS

★ ★ ★

Create a PowerPoint Presentation or Blog

What's So Cool About California?

Pick 10 of California's most interesting natural landmarks. What geographical features make them unique? Power up your presentation with:

★ A map showing their geographic locations and regions.

★ Photos, illustrations, tourism posters and brochures, Web links.

★ Cool natural history facts, your own "WOW factor" geographic stats, climate and weather, plant life and wildlife, recent discoveries.

SEE: Chapter One, pages 8–23.

GO TO: California's Web site www.ca.gov to download and print maps and photos. Call 800/GO-CALIF for a *California Visitors Guide Magazine* and brochures as references.

State Quarter Project

From 1999 to 2008, the U.S. Mint introduced new quarters commemorating each of the 50 states in the order that they were admitted to the Union. Each state's quarter features a unique design on its back, or reverse.

★ Research the significance of each image.

★ Who designed the quarter?

★ Who chose the final design?

★ Design your own California quarter. What images would you choose for the reverse?

★ Make a poster showing the California quarter and label each image.

GO TO: www.usmint.gov/kids and find out what's featured on the back of the California quarter.

Write a Journal or Diary

Picture Yourself . . .

★ trailblazing with mountain man James Beckwourth or Jedediah Smith. Write a journal of your travels.

SEE: Chapter Four, pages 44–45.

★ as a member of the Donner Party who survives the deadly journey from Illinois to California by wagon train from 1846–1847. Write a "Westward Ho" survival guide for future travelers.

SEE: Chapter Four, page 46.

★ as a participant in a boycott led by labor activist César Chávez.

SEE: Chapter Five, page 67.

GO TO: Visit the United Farm Workers' Web site at www.ufw.org to find out about issues facing farmworkers today. Write an editorial for your school or local paper taking a pro or con position on an issue.

ART PROJECTS

★ ★ ★

Create a Diorama
Stuck in Tar or Traffic?

Create a two-sided diorama! One side shows the original site of the La Brea Tar Pits thousands of years ago with animals trapped in the goo. The other side shows what's there now—the busy Miracle Mile district in Los Angeles that's home to the Tar Pits museum!

SEE: See It Here! La Brea Tar Pits on page 113.

GO TO: www.tarpits.org, the Page Museum, for more information on the La Brea Tar Pits. Call and see if you can interview a scientist or paleontologist!

Illustrate the Lyrics to the State Song
I Love You, California!

Use markers, paints, photos, collage, colored pencils, or computer graphics to illustrate the lyrics to "I Love You, California." Turn your illustrations into a picture book or scan them into a PowerPoint presentation and add music!

SEE: Lyrics on page 128.

Build a Mission
Okay, So You Have to Build a Mission.

Here are some great resources to jump-start your research!

Book

Nelson, Libby, and Kari A. Cornell. *Projects and Layouts* (California Mission). Minneapolis: Lerner, 1998.

Web Sites

California Mission History
 www.californiamissions.com

California Mission Internet Trail
 www.eusd4kids.org/mission_trail/ MissionTrail.html

California Missions Interactive
 www.tsoft.net/~cmi/index.html#Buttons

More California Mission History
 www.californiamissions.com/ morehistory/

Mission-building Supplies

Pacific Coast Floral & Craft Supply
 www.createamission.com

Hobbylinc
 www.hobbylinc.com/htm/hca/ hca19020h.htm

SCIENCE, TECHNOLOGY, & MATH PROJECTS

★ ★ ★

Graph Earthquakes

Quake Shake Graphs

Read about California earthquakes on pages 20–21. Then research the strongest quakes that have hit the state. You can create a graph showing the seismic impact of these major quakes. Create a quake map to show their locations.

24/7 Shake Updates

California can have many small earthquakes a day! The U.S. Geological Survey (USGS) has a site that updates the exact location and intensity of each quake, 24/7!

GO TO: neic.usgs.gov/neis/last_event_states/states_california.html to see if a quake occurred in California today—and where! Make a graph of your findings over the course of a month. What fault lines are they near? Based on your findings, what quake predictions can you make?

GO TO: earthquake.usgs.gov/shakemap/ for ShakeMaps and other cool information about quakes.

Write a Letter or Report

Great Minds, Great Finds

Think about some of the scientists, explorers, and inventors you've read about in this book. Choose 1 or 2 you would like to meet. From blue jeans maker Levi Strauss to James Marshall, who discovered gold at Sutter's Mill, to seismologist Keiiti Aki to computer whizzes Steve Jobs and Steve Wozniak! Write a letter detailing why their discovery or scientific and technological achievements will continue to touch the lives of generations to come.

SEE: Mini-bios throughout this book.

GO TO: Biographical Dictionary on pages 133–136.

Track Endangered Species

Using your knowledge of California's wildlife, research what animals and plants are endangered or threatened.

★ Find out what the state is doing to protect these species.

★ Chart known populations of the animals and plants, and report on changes in certain geographical areas.

SEE: Chapter One, page 17.

GO TO: The U.S. Fish and Wildlife site at http://ecos.fws.gov/tess_public/StateListing.do?status=listed&state=CA or other California-specific sites such as www.endangeredspecie.com/states/ca.htm

PRIMARY VS. SECONDARY SOURCES

★ ★ ★

What's the Diff?

Your teacher may require at least one or two primary sources and one or two secondary sources for your assignment. So, what's the difference between the two?

★ **Primary sources are original.** You are reading the actual words of someone's diary, journal, letter, autobiography, or interview. Primary sources can also be photographs, maps, prints, cartoons, news/film footage, posters, first-person newspaper articles, drawings, musical scores, and recordings. By the way, when you conduct a survey, interview someone, shoot a video, or take photographs to include in a project—you are creating primary sources!

★ **Secondary sources are what you find in encyclopedias, textbooks, articles, biographies, and almanacs**. These are written by a person or group of people who tell about something that happened to someone else. Secondary sources also recount what another person said or did. This book is an example of a secondary source.

Now that you know what primary sources are—where can you find them?

★ **Your school or local library:** Check the library catalog for collections of original writings, government documents, musical scores, and so on. Some of this material may be stored on microfilm. The Library of Congress Web site (www.loc.gov) is an excellent online resource for primary source materials.

★ **Historical societies:** These organizations keep historical documents, photographs, and other materials. Staff members can help you find what you are looking for. History museums are also great places to see primary sources firsthand.

★ **The Internet:** There are lots of sites that have primary sources you can download and use in a project or assignment.

TIMELINE

★ ★ ★

U.S. Events `1500` **California Events**

1542
Juan Rodríguez Cabrillo explores San Diego Bay.

1565
Spanish admiral Pedro Menéndez de Avilés founds St. Augustine, Florida, the oldest continuously occupied European settlement in the continental United States.

1579
Francis Drake claims California for England.

`1600` **1602**
Sebastián Vizcaíno urges Spain to colonize California.

1607
The first permanent English settlement is established in North America at Jamestown.

`1700`

1769
Junípero Serra establishes the first mission at San Diego.

1776
Thirteen American colonies declare their independence from Britain, marking the beginning of the Revolutionary War.

1776
Spanish settlers from Mexico reach the site of present-day San Francisco.

`1800`

1803
The Louisiana Purchase almost doubles the size of the United States.

1812–15
The United States and Britain fight the War of 1812.

1812
Russian fur traders build Fort Ross.

1821
California becomes part of Mexico.

1830
The Indian Removal Act forces eastern Native American groups to relocate west of the Mississippi River.

1841
The first organized group of U.S. settlers reach California by land.

U.S. Events

1846–48

The United States fights a war with Mexico over western territories in the Mexican War.

1848

The first Women's Rights Convention meets in Seneca Falls, New York.

1868

The U.S. Congress approves the Fourteenth Amendment to the U.S. Constitution, granting citizenship to African Americans.

1917–18

The United States is involved in World War I.

1920

The Nineteenth Amendment to the U.S. Constitution grants women the right to vote.

1941–45

The United States engages in World War II.

California Events

1846

The Bear Flag of the California Republic is raised over Sonoma.

1848

Gold is discovered at Sutter's Mill, in present-day Coloma.

1849

The gold rush begins.

1850

California becomes a state.

1887

Population growth causes a land boom in Southern California.

1900

1906

A major earthquake and fire partially destroy San Francisco.

1915

Expositions in San Diego and San Francisco mark the opening of the Panama Canal.

1924

Japanese immigration is ended.

1937

Construction of the Golden Gate Bridge is completed.

1942

President Franklin D. Roosevelt authorizes the removal of all people of Japanese descent along the West Coast to internment camps.

U.S. Events

California Events

1945
The U.N. Charter is adopted in San Francisco.

1951–53
The United States engages in the Korean War.

1963
California becomes the most populous state.

1964–73
The United States engages in the Vietnam War.

1975
Migrant farmworkers obtain the right to collective bargaining.

1984
The Summer Olympic Games are held in Los Angeles.

1988
The U.S. Congress approves the payment of monetary compensation to Japanese Americans interned during World War II.

1989
An earthquake strikes San Francisco, Oakland, and San Jose.

1991
The United States and other nations fight the brief Persian Gulf War against Iraq.

1994
A strong earthquake strikes Los Angeles.

2000

2001
Terrorists hijack four U.S. aircraft and crash them into the World Trade Center in New York City, the Pentagon in Washington, D.C., and a Pennsylvania field, killing thousands.

2003
The United States and coalition forces invade Iraq.

2003
Arnold Schwarzenegger is elected governor when Gray Davis is recalled from office.

2007
San Francisco congresswoman Nancy Pelosi becomes the first female Speaker of the House.

GLOSSARY

abolitionist a person who works to end slavery

adobe bricks made of sun-dried clay; also, a house made with these bricks

amendments changes to a law or legal document

appeal a legal proceeding in which a court is asked to change the decision of a lower court

boycotts refusals, usually planned by a group, to buy certain products or use certain services

chaparral a thicket of dense shrubs, bushes, and small trees

charter a basic set of rules

colony a territory claimed by the country that settles it

conifers trees that bear cones

constitution a written document that contains all the governing principles of a state or country

dormant not active at present, but could be active at some future time

fugitive a person who tries to flee or escape

Great Depression an economic downturn in U.S. history (1929 through 1939) when many people lost their jobs and suffered financial difficulties

incorporated recognized as a self-governing entity

internment camps places where large groups of people are confined, usually during a war

lava fiery melted rock

legislature the lawmaking body for a state or country

missions places where people teach their religion to others

rituals religious ceremonies or social customs

strikes organized refusals to work

tallow hard fat from the bodies of cattle or other animals

transcontinental crossing an entire continent, or landmass between oceans

FAST FACTS

State Symbols

Statehood date	September 9, 1850, the 31st state
Origin of state name	Named by Spanish explorers after California, the mythical island paradise in Garci Rodríguez de Montalvo's 16th-century book, *Sergas de Esplandián* (The Exploits of Esplandián)
State capital	Sacramento
State nickname	Golden State
State motto	Eureka, or "I have found it!"
State bird	California valley quail
State flower	Golden poppy
State fish	Golden trout
State rock	Serpentine
State gem	Benitoite
State song	"I Love You, California" (see p. 128 for lyrics)
State tree	California redwood
State fossil	Saber-toothed cat
State insect	California dog-face butterfly
State fair	Sacramento, August

State flag

Geography

Total area; rank	163,696 square miles (423,973 sq km); 3rd
Land; rank	155,959 square miles (403,934 sq km); 3rd
Water; rank	7,736 square miles (20,036 sq km); 6th
Inland water	2,674 square miles (6,926 sq km)
Coastal water	222 square miles (575 sq km)
Territorial water	4,841 square miles (12,538 sq km)
Geographic center	Madera County, 38 miles (61 km) east of Madera
Latitude and Longitude	114° 8' W to 124° 24' W 32° 30' N to 42° N
Highest point	Mount Whitney, 14,505 feet (4,421 m)
Lowest point	Death Valley, 282 feet (86 m) below sea level
Largest city	Los Angeles
Number of counties	58
Longest river	Sacramento

State capitol

Population

Population; rank (2006 estimate)	36,457,549; 1st
Density (2006 estimate)	223 persons per sq. mi. (86 per sq km)
Population distribution (2000 census)	94% urban, 6% rural
Race (2005 estimate)	White persons: 77.0%*
	Asian persons: 12.2%*
	Black persons: 6.7%*
	American Indian and Alaska Native persons: 1.2%*
	Native Hawaiian and Other Pacific Islanders: 0.4%*
	Persons reporting two or more races: 2.4%*
	Persons of Hispanic or Latino origin: 35.2%†
	White persons, not Hispanic: 43.8%

Includes persons reporting only one race
† Hispanics may be of any race, so they are also included in applicable race categories.

Weather

Record high temperature	134°F (57°C) at Greenland Ranch on July 10, 1913
Record low temperature	−45°F (−43°C) at Boca on January 20, 1973
Average July temperature, Los Angeles	69°F (21°C)
Average January temperature, Los Angeles	57°F (14°C)
Average yearly precipitation, Los Angeles	13 in. (33 cm)
Average July temperature, San Francisco	63°F (17°C)
Average January temperature, San Francisco	49°F (9°C)
Average yearly precipitation, San Francisco	20 in. (51 cm)

State seal

Golden trout

STATE SONG

"I Love You, California"

Words by F. B. Silverwood; Music by A. F. Frankenstein

California's official state song was written by F. B. Silverwood, a Los Angeles merchant. The words were put to music by Alfred Frankenstein, a former conductor for the Los Angeles Symphony Orchestra. It was the official song of expositions held in San Francisco and San Diego in 1915, and it was played aboard the first ship to go through the Panama Canal. In 1951, the state legislature passed a resolution designating it as California's state song.

I love you, California, you're the greatest state of all;
I love you in the winter, summer, spring, and in fall;
I love your fertile valleys; your dear mountains I adore;
I love your grand old ocean and I love her rugged shore.

(Chorus)
Where the snow-crowned Golden Sierras
Keep their watch o'er the valleys bloom,
It is there I would be in our land by the sea,
Ev'ry breeze bearing rich perfume,
It is here nature gives of her rarest
It is Home Sweet Home to me,
And I know when I die I shall breathe my last sigh
For my sunny California.

I love your redwood forests—love your fields of yellow grain;
I love your summer breezes and I love your winter rain;
I love you, land of flowers; land of honey, fruit and wine;
I love you, California; you have won this heart of mine.

(Chorus)
I love your old gray Missions—love your vineyards stretching far;
I love you, California, with your Golden Gate ajar;
I love your purple sunsets, love your skies of azure blue;
I love you, California; I just can't help loving you.

(Chorus)
I love you, California, you are very dear to me;
I love you, Tamalpais, and I love Yosemite;
I love you, Land of Sunshine, half your beauties are untold;
I loved you in my childhood, and I'll love you when I'm old.

NATURAL AREAS AND HISTORIC SITES

★ ★ ★

National Parks

California's eight national parks are among the most visited in the nation, including *Yosemite National Park, Redwood National Park, Joshua Tree National Park, Kings Canyon National Park, Death Valley National Park,* and *Sequoia National Park.*

National Seashore

Point Reyes National Seashore is about 40 miles (64 km) from San Francisco.

National Monuments

Five national monuments are in California, including *Lava Beds National Monument,* which is home to 500 underground lava-tube caves.

National Historic Trails

Four historic trails cross parts of California, including *California National Historic Trail,* which follows a portion of the 5,500-mile (8,850-km) route that pioneers and gold miners took to the West.

National Historical Park

San Francisco Maritime National Historical Park has a fine collection of historic vessels, a library, and a maritime museum.

National Historic Sites

California is home to four national historic sites, including *Manzanar National Historic Site,* which is the site of the Manzanar Relocation Center, where persons of Japanese heritage were interned during World War II.

Other sites protected by the National Park Service

California has three national recreation areas, including *Golden Gate National Recreational Area,* one of the world's largest urban parks. Both the *Presidio*—a strategic military location for the U.S. Navy—and *Alcatraz Island* are in the Bay Area.

National Forests

California has 18 national forests covering 20 million acres (8.1 million ha).

State Parks and Forests

The California state park system includes more than 270 sites. The largest is the *Anza-Borrego Desert State Park,* which covers 600,000 acres (243,000 ha) of desert and mountains. *Humboldt Redwoods State Park* is perhaps the best known of the state parks that preserve stands of redwood trees. California has eight state forests.

SPORTS TEAMS

★ ★ ★

NCAA Teams (Division I)

California Polytechnic State University *Mustangs*

California State University–Fresno *Bulldogs*

California State University–Fullerton *Titans*

California State University–Northridge *Matadors*

California State University–Sacramento *Hornets*

Long Beach State University *49ers*

Loyola Marymount University *Lions*

Pepperdine University *Waves*

Saint Mary's College *Gaels*

San Diego State University *Aztecs*

San Jose State University *Spartans*

Santa Clara University *Broncos*

Stanford University *Cardinal*

University of California–Berkeley *Golden Bears*

University of California–Davis *Aggies*

University of California–Irvine *Anteaters*

University of California–Los Angeles *Bruins*

University of California–Riverside *Highlanders*

University of California–Santa Barbara *Gauchos*

University of the Pacific *Tigers*

University of San Diego *Toreros*

University of San Francisco *Dons*

University of Southern California *Trojans*

PROFESSIONAL SPORTS TEAMS

★ ★ ★

Major League Baseball
Anaheim Angels
Los Angeles Dodgers
Oakland Athletics
San Diego Padres
San Francisco Giants

Major League Soccer
LA Galaxy

National Basketball Association
Golden State Warriors
Los Angeles Clippers
Los Angeles Lakers
Sacramento Kings

Women's National Basketball Association
Los Angeles Sparks
Sacramento Monarchs

National Football League
Oakland Raiders
San Diego Chargers
San Francisco 49ers

Hockey
Los Angeles Kings
San Jose Sharks
Mighty Ducks of Anaheim

CULTURAL INSTITUTIONS

Libraries

Bancroft Library (University of California–Berkeley), *California State Library* (Sacramento), and the *Library of the California Historical Society* (San Francisco) all have important collections on California's history.

San Francisco Public Library and *Los Angeles Public Library* are the state's most extensive public library systems.

Museums

California African American Museum (Los Angeles) explores the history, culture, and art of African Americans in the western United States.

California Science Center (Los Angeles) is the West Coast's largest hands-on science center.

Chinese American Museum (Los Angeles) highlights the contributions Chinese Americans have made.

Crocker Art Museum (Sacramento), *J. Paul Getty Museum* (Malibu), and *M. H. De Young Memorial Museum* (San Francisco) all have important art works.

Henry E. Huntington Library and Art Gallery (San Marino) contains extensive collections of European art, furniture, and porcelain.

Los Angeles County Museum of Art is the largest art museum in the western United States.

Universities and Colleges

In 2006, California had 141 public and 209 private institutions of higher learning.

The University of California system includes 10 campuses, more than 209,000 students and 170,000 faculty and staff.

California State University has 23 campuses, 417,000 students, and 46,000 faculty and staff.

ANNUAL EVENTS

January–March

Chinese New Year celebration in San Francisco and Los Angeles (January, February, or March)

Whiskey Flat Days in Kernville (February)

Swallows return to San Juan Capistrano (March)

April–June

Aleutian Goose Festival in Crescent City (April)

Northern California Cherry Blossom Festival in San Francisco (April)

High Desert Arts Festival in Ridgecrest (April)

Long Beach Grand Prix (April)

Godwit Days Bird Migration Festival in Arcata (April)

Red Bluff Round-Up in Red Bluff (April)

Stockton Asparagus Festival (April)

Calaveras County Fair & Jumping Frog Jubilee in Angels Camp (May)

Cinco de Mayo in Los Angeles (May)

Kinetic Sculpture Race from Arcata to Ferndale (May)

Oakdale Chocolate Festival (May)

Sacramento Jazz Jubilee (May)

Salinas Valley Fair in King City (May)

Strawberry Festival in Galt (May)

Semana Nautica, a summer sports festival, in Santa Barbara (June–July)

July–September

California WorldFest in Grass Valley (July)

Fortuna Rodeo (July)

Mozart Festival in San Luis Obispo (July)

Santa Barbara National Horse Show (July)

Shakespeare Santa Cruz (July–August)

Scottish Games and Celtic Festival in Monterey (early August)

Old Spanish Days Fiesta in Santa Barbara (early August)

State Fair in Sacramento (August–September)

African Marketplace and Cultural Faire in Los Angeles (August–September)

Lodi Grape Festival and Harvest Fair (September)

Long Beach Blues Festival (September)

Monterey Jazz Festival (September)

Stater Bros. Route 66 Rendezvous® in San Bernardino (September)

Oktoberfest at Big Bear Lake (mid-September to late October)

October–December

Clam Festival in Pismo Beach (October)

Lone Pine Film Festival (October)

Christmas Boat Parade in Newport Beach (December)

Christmas Festival of Lights in Fortuna (December)

BIOGRAPHICAL DICTIONARY

Ansel Adams (1902–1984) was a photographer famous for his dramatic black-and-white photos of the American West, especially the Sierra Nevada and Yosemite Valley. He was born in San Francisco.

Keiiti Aki See page 20.

Luis Walter Alvarez (1911–1988) was a physicist at the University of California in Berkeley. Alvarez won the 1968 Nobel Prize in Physics. He was born in San Francisco.

Maya Angelou (1928–) is known for her poetry and autobiographical writing, including *I Know Why the Caged Bird Sings*. But before she became a successful author, she tried many jobs. She was born in Missouri, but as a teen, she was San Francisco's first-ever African American cable car conductor.

Judith Baca (1946–) is a Mexican American artist, activist, and professor, responsible for *The Great Wall of Los Angeles*, the longest mural in the world.

Patricia Bath (1942–) is a skilled surgeon and an inventor. One of her patented medical inventions—a laser that's used to remove cataracts from the eyes—has saved the eyesight of many people.

James Beckwourth See page 45.

Susan Billy See page 31.

Shirley Temple Black See page 63.

Tom Bradley See page 69.

Sam Brannon (1819–1889) made a small fortune during the gold rush by selling supplies to people mining for gold.

Luther Burbank (1849–1926) was a man with the proverbial "green thumb." He grew up on a farm in Massachusetts and, in 1875, went to California and set up a plant nursery. Over the course of his life, he developed almost 400 new species of fruits, vegetables, grasses, and flowers.

César Chávez See page 67.

Margaret Cho (1968–) is an award-winning stand-up comic and writer. She was born in San Francisco.

Louise Amelia Knapp Smith Clappe (1819–1906) was one of the few women to live in a California mining camp. In 1851, she began writing letters to her sister. These letters are full of humor and great detail about camp life. Later, using the pen name Dame Shirley, Clappe published her letters.

Margaret Cho

Coolio (1963–) is a musician whose best-known hit is "Gangsta's Paradise." He was born in Compton as Artis Leon Ivey Jr. His friends called him Coolio after the singer Julio Iglesias.

Leonardo DiCaprio (1974–) is an actor who starred in *Titanic* (1997), *The Aviator* (2004), and other films. He was born in Hollywood.

Joe DiMaggio (1914–1999) Baseball legend. A New York Yankee, his 56-game hitting streak in 1941 was the longest in history. He was born in Martinez.

Walt Disney See page 114.

Yen Ngoc Do (1941–2006) was a Vietnamese immigrant who began publishing the *Nguoi Viet Daily News* newspaper in 1978 for people like himself who were adjusting to life in their new country. Now, 17,000 people throughout the United States read it each day.

Amelia Earhart (1897–1937) was an aviator and the first woman to fly solo across the Atlantic Ocean. She was born in Kansas, but learned to fly in California.

Frank Epperson (1894–1983) of Oakland invented the Popsicle in 1905. At the time, he was just 11 years old.

Jaime Escalante See page 79.

March Fong Eu (1922–), a third-generation Californian, started out running for a seat on the local school board and ended up being elected California's secretary of state.

Dian Fossey (1932–1985) studied the behavior of gorillas for years in the mountain forests of Rwanda. She was born in San Francisco.

Robert Frost (1874–1963) was a leading American poet and the winner of four Pulitzer Prizes for poetry. Among his best-loved poems is "Stopping by Woods on a Snowy Evening." Frost was born in San Francisco.

Jerry Garcia (1942–1995) was the guitarist and lead singer in the rock band the Grateful Dead. Garcia was born in San Francisco.

Mifflin Wistar Gibbs See page 54.

Allen Ginsberg (1926–1997) was a San Francisco poet who was part of the Beat Generation.

Charles P. Ginsburg (1920–1992) led the research team that developed the first videotape recorder. This led TV studios to switch from live to recorded shows. Ginsburg was born in San Francisco.

William Randolph Hearst (1863–1951) was the owner of a number of newspapers, including the *San Francisco Examiner*. He was born in San Francisco, and his palatial estate, Hearst Castle, is located near San Simeon.

Dolores Huerta (1930–) cofounded the NFWA with César Chávez in 1962. Huerta was inducted into the National Women's Hall of Fame in 1993, and she received the Eleanor Roosevelt Award from President Bill Clinton in 1998.

Steve Jobs (1955–) was born in San Francisco. He and Steve Wozniak created the Apple computer.

Earvin "Magic" Johnson See page 103.

Jimmie Johnson (1975–) is a champion race-car driver. Born in El Cajon.

Nancy Kelsey (1823–1896) was the first white woman to reach California overland.

Billie Jean King (1943–) is a Hall of Fame tennis great from Long Beach. She formed the Women's Tennis Association in 1973.

Michelle Kwan (1980–) is the most successful figure skater in U.S. history. By 2006, she had won nine U.S. championships and five world championships, as well as silver (1988) and bronze (2002) medals in the Olympic Games. Kwan was born in Torrance.

Dorothea Lange (1895–1965) was a photographer and filmmaker best known for her work during the Great Depression. She was born in New Jersey, but moved to San Francisco in 1918.

George Lucas (1944–) is a filmmaker who created the *Star Wars* movies. He was born in Modesto.

Steve Jobs

Theodore Harold Maiman (1927–) invented the first practical laser, in 1960. Maiman was born in Los Angeles.

Norman Yoshio Mineta See page 65.

Marilyn Monroe (1926–1962) was a glamorous Hollywood movie star of the 1950s. She was born Norma Jean Baker in Los Angeles.

Julia Morgan (1872–1957) was an architect who had a reputation for really listening to her clients and making their ideas a reality. One of her biggest projects was Hearst Castle.

John Muir See page 14.

Richard Milhous Nixon See page 90.

Isamu Noguchi (1904–1988) was a Japanese American sculptor who combined traditional Japanese styles with modern art. He was born in Los Angeles.

Ellen Ochoa (1958–) is an astronaut who has flown four space shuttle missions. The first Hispanic woman in space, she was born in Los Angeles.

Ellen Ochoa

Nancy Pelosi See page 90.

Leo Politi (1908–1996) is a children's book author and illustrator. He is best known for portraying children in Los Angeles's multicultural neighborhoods.

Ronald Wilson Reagan See page 90.

Robert Redford (1936–) is an actor and director. He starred in *Butch Cassidy and the Sundance Kid* (1970) and dozens of other films.

Granville Redmond (1871–1935) was one of California's most respected landscape architects.

Sally Ride (1951–) is an astronaut who became the first American woman in space. She was born in Encino.

David Laughing Horse Robinson (1955–) ran for governor in 2003, becoming the first Native American to run for statewide office. He is also an artist and an expert on ancient rock art.

Garci Rodriguez de Montalvo (1450?–1510?) was a Spanish writer whose 1510 novel *Las Sergas de Esplandián* (The Exploits of Esplandián) described a mythical island called California.

Lucille Roybal-Allard (1941–) was the first Mexican American woman elected to Congress. As a member of the House of Representatives, she served citizens of the 34th District of California, which includes downtown Los Angeles. She was born in Boyle Heights.

Pam Muñoz Ryan (1951–) writes books for children and young adults. Her novel *Esperanza Rising* tells about her grandmother's childhood experiences. She was born in Bakersfield.

Jonas Salk (1914–1995) was a doctor and researcher who invented the polio vaccine in 1955. It prevented millions of children from getting the crippling disease. He founded the Salk Institute for Biological Studies in La Jolla. He was born in New York City.

Carlos Santana (1947–) is an award-winning musician and Latin-rock guitarist. He was born in Mexico and moved to San Francisco.

Dalip Singh Saund (1899–1973) was the first Asian American and first Indian American to serve in the U.S. Congress. Born in India, he moved to California and served in the U.S. House of Representatives from 1951 to 1963.

Arnold Schwarzenegger See page 89.

Father Junípero Serra See page 37.

Jedediah Smith See page 44.

Brenda Song (1988–) is an actor who has appeared in a number of Disney projects and the film *Like Mike*. She was born in Carmichael.

Gary Soto See page 82.

Jane Stanford (1828–1905) cofounded Stanford University with her husband, Leland, and helped the school grow after his death. She advocated admitting women students long before the policy was popular.

Leland Stanford (1824–1893) was a New York-born lawyer who moved to California. He helped build the Transcontinental Railroad and cofounded Stanford University.

John Steinbeck (1902–1968) was the author of *In Dubious Battle* and *The Grapes of Wrath*. He was born in Salina.

Levi Strauss See page 57.

Amy Tan (1952–) writes about Chinese culture and the struggles of Chinese Americans. One of her best-known books is *The Joy Luck Club*. She was born in Oakland.

Antonio Villaraigosa (1953–) was elected mayor of Los Angeles in 2005.

Alice Walker (1944–) is the Pulitzer Prize–winning author of *The Color Purple*. She lives in northern California.

Earl Warren (1891–1974) served as governor of California and later as chief justice of the U.S. Supreme Court. He grew up in Bakersfield.

Alice Waters See page 80.

Alice Walker

Venus (1980–) and Serena (1981–) Williams are world-champion tennis players. Serena was born in Michigan and Venus in Lynwood, California. They grew up in Compton.

Laurence Yep

Brian Wilson (1942–) is a songwriter and musician who cofounded and led the Beach Boys. In the 1960s, this band glorified Southern California's surfer lifestyle with songs such as "Surfer Girl" and "Surfin' USA." He was born in Hawthorne.

Eldrick "Tiger" Woods see page 83.

Jerry Yang (1951–) is a computer whiz. Born in Taiwan. While at Stanford University, he and a classmate created Yahoo!—now the world's most-visited Web site.

Laurence Yep (1948–) writes fantasy and science-fiction novels for young people. His books include *Dragonwings*, *Dragon's Gate*, and the Tiger's Apprentice series. A Chinese American, Yep was born in San Francisco.

Al Young (1939–) is a poet who portrays many aspects of the African American experience. From 2005 to 2007, he served as the state's poet laureate.

Frank Zamboni (1901–1988) perfected the ice resurfacer. He and his brother built the Iceland Skating Rink in Paramount.

RESOURCES

BOOKS

Nonfiction

Corwin, Judith Hoffman. *Native American Crafts of California, the Great Basin, and the Southwest*. Danbury, Conn.: Franklin Watts, 2002.

Cosson, M. J. *Welcome to Redwood National Park*. Chanhassen, Minn.: The Child's World, 2006.

Keremitsis, Eileen. *Life in a California Mission*. San Diego: Lucent Books, 2002.

Locker, Thomas. *John Muir: America's Naturalist*. Golden, Colo.: Fulcrum Books, 2003.

Murphy, Claire Rudolf. *Children of Alcatraz: Growing Up on the Rock*. New York: Walker Books for Young Readers, 2006.

Olmstead. Mary. *Judy Baca*. Chicago: Raintree, 2005.

Rosinsky, Natalie M. *California Ranchos*. Mankato, Minn.: Compass Point Books, 2006.

Stein, R. Conrad. *The California Gold Rush*. Danbury, Conn.: Children's Press, 1995.

Wadsworth, Ginger. *Julia Morgan: Architect of Dreams*. Minneapolis: Lerner, 1990.

Yamane, Linda. *Weaving a California Tradition: A Native American Basketmaker*. Minneapolis: Lerner, 1996.

Yep, Laurence. *The Earth Dragon Awakes: The San Francisco Earthquake of 1906*. New York: HarperCollins, 2006.

Fiction

Fletcher, Susan. *Walk Across the Sea*. New York: Atheneum, 2001.

Johnston, Tony. *Any Small Goodness: A Novel of the Barrio*. New York: Blue Sky Press, 2001.

Krensky, Stephen. *The Iron Dragon Never Sleeps*. New York: Delacorte Books for Young Readers, 1994.

Marsh, Carol. *The Mystery on the California Mission Trail*. Peachtree City, Ga.: Gallopade International, 2003.

O'Dell, Scott. *The Black Pearl*. Boston: Houghton Mifflin, 1967.

Ryan, Pamela Muñoz. *Esperanza Rising*. New York: Scholastic, 2002.

Soto, Gary. *Petty Crimes*. San Diego: Harcourt, 1998.

DVDs

American Experience: The Great San Francisco Earthquake. WGBH Boston, 2005.

Big Sur: California Coast. Image Entertainment, 2002.

California's Parks and Monuments. Finley-Holiday Film Corporation, 2005.

Modern Marvels: Los Angeles. A&E Home Video, 2006.

Ten Days That Unexpectedly Changed the World: Gold Rush. A&E Home Video, 2006.

WEB SITES AND ORGANIZATIONS

California Historical Society

www.californiahistoricalsociety.org
678 Mission Street
San Francisco, CA 94105
415/357-1848
Explore California's history online and learn about the many exhibits at the historical society

California Secretary of State

www.ss.ca.gov
The official Web site of the California secretary of state, including the secretary's events calendar and link portals to online services

California Tourism

http://gocalif.ca.gov/state/tourism/tour_ homepage.jsp
A statewide guide to tourism and recreational events and activities

California State Capitol Museum

www.capitolmuseum.ca.gov
11th and L Streets
Sacramento, CA 95812
916/324-0333
A complete guide to the capitol and its rich history

California Department of Parks and Recreation

www.parks.ca.gov
1416 9th Street
Sacramento, CA 95814
800/777-0369
A complete guide to California's many state parks

INDEX

★ ★ ★

AUTHOR'S TIPS AND SOURCE NOTES

★   ★   ★

California always held an allure for me, so researching this book was a pleasure. I consulted the usual sources—making lots and lots of trips to the library and onto the Internet for numbers and facts—but I also watched a few DVDs about the state and had fun going to Google and typing in "California trivia and odd facts." I just never knew what would come up!

There are some great sites. I recommend checking out www.isu.edu/~trinmich/funfacts.html for some neat stuff about California's history. Reading about the Donner Party was not fun—but it was still very interesting and worth learning more about, just to see the incredible heart and determination of human beings. For some additional great trivia about the state, check out www.50states.com/facts/calif.htm.